the SPROUTED KITCHEN

BOWL+SPOON

the SPROUTED KITCHEN
BOWL+SPOON

_____

simple and inspired whole foods recipes to savor and share

Sara Forte

photography by Hugh Forte

TEN SPEED PRESS
Berkeley

For Curran
We hope for you a life of taking risks and doing what brings you joy. You inspire us to live out that example for you. This book is just as much yours as it is ours. We're so excited to have you at our table, sweet boy.

Contents

BIG BOWLS

SWEET BOWLS

DRESSING AND SAUCES

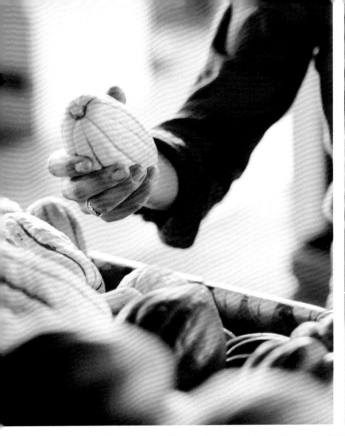

Overview

The seed for this book was planted by an indirect compliment from my husband, Hugh, about my cooking. Knowing I was an enthusiastic home cook, someone had asked him what my "specialty" was. He and I both know I don't necessarily have a favorite cuisine. Through trial, error, and money wasted, I'm mediocre at cooking meat. I am too unconventional for perfect baking and err on the side of health nut for classical dishes. What I do well is what I care most about, which is produce.

I have an affinity for seasonal vegetables and whole foods with bold dressings or sauces. I crave healthful, colorful foods that taste good. My specialty, per se, is food in a bowl—combinations of vegetables, whole grains, lean proteins, big salads—texture and flavor that go together to make a simple, nutritious meal that makes sense composed in one vessel. "Bowl foods" was Hugh's answer to the question. First I took offense, then I laughed about it, and after telling the story, I came to realize that this is the way a lot of whole foods–focused eaters cook: a dish colorful enough to serve when friends are over for dinner, the kind of meal you can bring to the couch with nothing but a spoon or fork, or where leftovers can be packed up easily for the following day. One could argue that food in a bowl has an aesthetic gentleness to it that feels stark on a plate—ingredients nestled within each other, tangled to make most sense as a sum of their parts. I am using the bowl as a point of inspiration for the recipes shared here.

I grew up in a home where eating together—but not necessarily cooking—was emphasized. We laugh about it now, especially given the style of food I lean toward, but most things were frozen, canned, or mixed from a packet. One of my mom's standbys was frozen taquitos sticking out of a bowl of microwaved Ranch Beans (they came in a can, sweet and barbeque-ish), or my dad made us blue box mac n cheese with hot dogs in it . . . and I am not referring to the organic, grass-fed kind.

My childhood is reflected upon fondly—I have great parents who made life fun and gave my sister and me every opportunity to succeed, but my career now is an ironic juxtaposition to the eating habits we had growing up.

I went to college in San Luis Obispo and, out of curiousity, started working at the organic farm on campus. I was paid in vegetables, and in my best effort to live on a budget, I taught myself how to cook given what I was sent home with. I watched shows, scoured magazines and cookbooks, and learned by trial and error. It was then that I fell in love with knowing where my food came from and how it was treated and tended to. I witnessed the full farm-to-table circle, firsthand, and cooking and eating became a lot more personal. Working on that farm, be it a small chapter of my life, is largely responsible for how passionate I am about seasonal produce today. I learned the stark difference between a fresh summer tomato and the kind you get from a conventional market in December—simple, nutritious food made sense when you paid brief attention to what was in season and timed it right.

After school, I took an internship in Tuscany, Italy, at an olive oil farm and cooking school called Villa Lucia. There, as seen in most of Italy, I learned more of the emphasis on using excellent ingredients and well-executed preparations to make uncomplicated, delicious food. I worked hard and woke up early to prepare breakfast for the guests. I watched and listened—that is how I have become a better cook, by watching and listening to what people like, how food makes them feel, what aesthetically makes them respond. To feed people is an act of service and generosity—there is more to it than just filling your belly. I dated and married my sweet husband among all this—a man who prefers cheeseburgers but loves to be fed regardless. He is a talented photographer and we started *Sprouted Kitchen*, a food journal, as a place to document thoughts on life, recipes, and his dynamic photos. We figured out how to work together as a team, amicably as possible, and in time, acquired opportunities for freelance work, teaching classes and workshops, and publishing two cookbooks.

Writers and entrepeneurs use the word *journey* loosely and often when referring to their careers, as this path proves surprising and unpredictable, but I really feel that is the best word to describe the ride Hugh and I are on with food writing and photography. It has led us to meet some incredible people and provide a lifestyle of doing work we enjoy. I aspire to always share pieces of a life being figured out alongside my delight in making food with those who share a similar enthusiasm for both. Having an online space to do so has been incredibly rewarding. We have a little boy who will be sharing a seat at our table as well. He's mini. I don't know if he'll prefer cheeseburgers or salad, but I'm excited to feed him.

Through feedback from journaling on *Sprouted Kitchen*, teaching classes, and consulting friends on dinner plans, I've found that the recipes people want are the ones I make as part of our everyday life. People are busy, time is limited, and while there are Sunday afternoons for a meal with a longer list of steps and more dishes to clean, the resounding request is practical—delicious, healthful, and practical. I am not classically trained nor do I have a culinary school degree on my resume. My experience and authority comes from feeding people and paying attention. My style is quite simple. It is colorful and thoughtful in its combination of textures, colors, and hints of flavor with cheese, nuts, or an herb-packed dressing—but it's simple to prepare. The advanced cook may find it overly so, but my goal is to speak to the everyday home cooks who desire to prepare wholesome, vibrant foods at their tables. I depend on using fresh, seasonal produce at its peak for the food to taste great in its natural state. Most instruction you will find here is straightforward and the ingredients easily found at a farmers' market, health food store, or wellstocked grocery store. There are phenomenal books that teach skills like braising, roasting, or grilling; you can even find ones on entertaining and crafting a lovely tablescape. While cooking as a hobby continues to grow in popularity, you will be able to find a cookbook on just about any facet of the process. But this book is a collection of recipes inspired by the marriage of flavor, color, texture, and wholesomeness that compose a dish—nestled in a bowl, in particular. The naysayer could argue a number of these recipes may also be served on a plate and I wouldn't disagree. The title is *bowl + spoon*, yet many are better eaten with a fork. In the name of cooking and pleasure, let's leave the literal and pragmatic aside. Much like painting or writing, the process of writing a cookbook is deciding on a thesis; and food in bowls, whether served family style or individually, is essentially the thesis of this cookbook.

We'll start with breakfast, of course, and continue with small bowls of sides and dips, then big bowls, which stand alone as an entrée, and seal the deal with a few sweet bites. I've included a number of my favorite dressings and sauces as well—something to have on hand when you're throwing a quick meal together. Whether you're looking for a crisp green salad for a dinner on the porch with friends or a hearty tortilla soup for a cold night in, there is something satisfying and healthful for everyone in here.

I am often asked about altering recipes to accommodate allergies or specific diets. If you cannot eat cheese, don't scratch a recipe for that reason. Adjust these recipes to accommodate how you cook and eat. If you can't do nuts and they're used as a topping or garnish, leave them off! I don't often follow recipes to a tee, and I expect the reader to take some authority here as well.

In a generation of busyness and schedules and desperate convenience, I hope to encourage people to eat at home with people they care about, to compose produce-focused meals, and to value their health, through the food choices they make. My contribution to that is accessible recipes that take more time to prepare than eating out or microwaving, but reward you with the joy there is in feeding people well. I'm honored you're reading this book and allowing me to share a piece of my life via the foods I cook for my family. We have to eat; it is a basic need. Inviting people to your table, be it online, through a book, or in a literal sense, is where the point of need and community get blurred into something quite beautiful.

Wishing you many great meals in good company.

Building a Kitchen to Cook in

Clutter and excess make me anxious, so I try to keep our kitchen stocked with the tools and ingredients we use often. While it takes time to acquire equipment and there is cost involved in stocking natural ingredients, having a full pantry is the most convenient route to wholesome, varied meals. Even when I have slim pickings, I can typically rally together a whole grain, beans, whatever veggies are in the crisper, and a simple dressing to make a meal. Below are some of the tools and ingredients I reach for most often.

RIMMED BAKING SHEETS—I prefer a heavy, stainless steel baking sheet for everything from cookies and toasted nuts to roasted potatoes. I don't have to worry about scratching these and they are easily lined with parchment for simpler cleanup.

CAST-IRON PAN—Although it requires a little more upkeep, cast iron retains and transfers heat beautifully for cooking. A 10- or 12-inch pan will cover you for frittatas, a stunning apple crisp, or offer a great sear on tofu strips. To maintain its natural nonstick coating, be sure not to use harsh soaps or abrasives when cleaning.

FOOD PROCESSOR—I have a 14-cup Cuisinart that, though large, allows me to make anything from party-size amounts of hummus to veggie burger dough to a plethora of salad dressings. I don't use it daily and it's a hassle to clean, but when you need one, there really is no substitute, which makes this beast completely worth the investment.

KNIVES—You really don't need those expensive sets with twenty different knives. It's just more to store, clean, and sharpen. If nothing else, keep a good quality, sharp chef's knife, santoku (a flat blade, general-purpose Japanese chef's knife), paring knife, and a small and large serrated. I don't pledge allegiance to one brand; I think it depends on the size and shape of your hands and how you chop. Just take good care of what you have.

KITCHEN SCISSORS—These are essentially just an extension of my knives. I use them to cut herbs, green onions, pizza. They are an indispensable kitchen tool and certainly something I would need on a desert island.

the sprouted kitchen bowl + spoon

PREP BOWLS—I like both glass and stainless steel. An assortment of sizes makes prep easier and most can fit in the fridge as needed. I consider ramekins, for both baking and prep, under this umbrella.

MICROPLANE (RASP) GRATER—Perfect for citrus zest and a delicate sprinkle of a hard cheese like Parmesan. They are inexpensive, come in a few sizes, and all work great.

JULIENNE PEELER—I have only become a fan in the past couple of years. It makes beautiful, thin strips of vegetables for salad, or it can be used to strip zucchini into a veggie noodle replacement for pasta. It's aesthetically pleasing to have delicate, consistent strips of vegetables, and the tool is small and easy to store.

A Whole Foods Pantry

I hesitate to define what "whole foods" really are, as the topics of nutrition and health seem to have their own sets of controversy. The goal is to cook meals made from ingredients in their most original state to avoid excess sugars, chemicals, and preservatives. My meals are not perfect. Sometimes I eat french fries and I have a sweet tooth, but wellness, for me, is doing the best you can to take care of yourself—physically, spiritually, and mentally. You live your life, eat a lot of greens, and stay intentional. That said, I've made a list of pantry and fridge staples that enable me to make wholesome meals whether I'm following a recipe or shooting from the hip. Most of these items can be found at well-stocked grocery stores, health food markets, or online.

SWEETENERS

AGAVE NECTAR—This liquid sweetener is made from the same plant tequila comes from. It's easy to find these days and has a similar texture to honey. It dissolves well in liquid, which makes it great for cocktails or iced tea. It's sweeter than natural cane sugar, so you'll use about half the amount of regular sugar.

HONEY—I try to buy our honey at the farmers' market to support local beekeepers and because its natural properties are said to help with seasonal allergies. Nutritionally, it offers vitamin B6 and vitamin C. You can purchase honey in a number of different flavor varieties, depending on the nectar source the bees visited. I don't notice too much of a difference, especially in cooking, so use whichever kind appeals to you. Look for raw, unprocessed honey so its natural minerals and enzymes, which are otherwise killed by heat processing, are still intact.

MAPLE SYRUP—No longer just for waffles and pancakes, this sweetener packs a lot of flavor and some nutritional value. It has minerals, iron, calcium, zinc, manganese, and potassium. I often use it in dressings and sauces where that smoky sweetness is welcomed. I usually use grade B, which has a deeper color and flavor than grade A. The latter will offer a more subtle sweetness. Real maple syrup is not cheap, but a little goes a long way.

the sprouted kitchen bowl + spoon

MUSCAVADO—This is likely my most often used dry sweetener. It comes in light and brown varieties, and I use it in place of brown sugar for cookies, oatmeal, crumble toppings, and such. It's less refined cane sugar, so the true molasses flavor is carried through. It's fairly moist, so is best kept in a cool, dry place in an airtight container. I go through it quickly and find buying it online the easiest and least expensive option.

NATURAL/ORGANIC CANE SUGAR—This is the closest thing to "regular sugar." It is unbleached and usually in organic form. You can find it at most grocery stores and certainly at health food stores. While you want to enjoy sugar in moderate quantities, this is a little less processed than white, granulated sugar, so I consider it a better alternative.

TURBINADO SUGAR—This golden, raw cane sugar comes in large, sparkling crystals. It can be used in equal measure to any other dry sweetener but does have a more coarse texture, even after baking, so I find it doesn't distribute quite as much sweetness.

COCONUT SUGAR—This is a dark, dry sugar made from the flower buds of a coconut palm. It has a deep caramel-like flavor and can be used in place of brown sugar. I like it stirred into coffee and in some baked goods where I value its caramel notes. It does change the color of baked items to a deeper brown and is pretty sandy in texture. I don't use it as an alternative to natural cane sugar as it's very absorbent and the two act differently in recipes.

OILS AND FATS

EXTRA-VIRGIN OLIVE OIL—It is by far the most frequently used fat in our house. I use "first cold-pressed extra-virgin olive oil." This oil is made from the first press of olives and can carry a variety of grassy, floral, or herbal notes, depending on the brand and origin. The price point can vary significantly, so I tend to keep a less expensive bottle around for baking or light sautéing and a nicer bottle for when I will really taste it—like salad dressing or bread dipping. Extra-virgin olive oil is a versatile, heart-healthy fat. There are arguments for not cooking with olive oil at high heat because the health benefits start to degrade and potentially harmful components form in their place. It also changes the flavor, so I try to use coconut, grapeseed, or organic cold-pressed safflower oil as alternatives if the food will be at a high heat for awhile. In this book, I most often suggest olive oil for convenience, but you can use a substitute as desired. Keep your olive oil in a cool, dry place, away from any heat source for optimum freshness.

ORGANIC UNREFINED COCONUT OIL—This saturated fat has made a comeback in the past few years for its health properties and its high smoke point, which allows you to cook with it at high temperatures for stir-fries and roasting. It does have a tropical aroma and natural sweetness, so I use it when those qualities are appreciated (think: roasted winter squash, not eggs). It is a solid at room temperature but melts quickly with a touch of heat.

GRAPESEED OR SAFFLOWER OIL—There is a time and place for a neutral oil with a high smoke point, and olive oil will not usually work in these circumstances. Neither contribute much nutritionally, but they are ideal for things like homemade aioli or Asian dressings. I attempt to stay away from canola oil as most canola seeds in the United States are genetically modified.

TOASTED SESAME OIL—I use this oil frequently with Asian-influenced recipes. It has a sweet, toasty flavor and can take high heat. It's great for dressings, marinades, sautéeing, or drizzling over steamed vegetables. It's assertive, so a little goes a long way.

NUT OILS—These are more expensive oils and have a short shelf life, but boy, are they delicious. I'll splurge on pistachio and walnut oil in the summer when I'm making a lot of green salads, as they make for beautifully fragrant and simple salad dressings with your vinegar of choice.

UNSALTED ORGANIC BUTTER—It's always best to use unsalted butter in recipes in order to control the salt. Buy organic whenever possible as it has a much cleaner, creamy flavor, and a more vibrant color, or at least buy a grass-fed version, if you can find it. It's a saturated fat, but in moderation, I consider it well worth the great flavor and texture it adds to food and baked goods. Buttered toast? I mean, even in a dairy-free phase, I can respect its greatness.

VINEGARS AND SALTS

VINEGARS—In order of most used: apple cider, red wine, white wine, rice wine, balsamic, white balsamic, and champagne vinegars. They are inexpensive and last forever, so keep a good collection on hand. Food needs acidity to balance sweetness, fat, and spice; different vinegars can round out flavors and brighten up a dish. If a dish tastes flat, a splash of acid and pinch of salt are sure to liven it up.

SEA SALT—I always use the same salt for consistency, as not all salts contribute the same salinity in cooking. Just find a brand you like and stay loyal to it, and you'll know precisely what a pinch or two pinches will do for your food. Sea salt is simply evaporated seawater as opposed to coming from a mine; however, the nutritional difference is said to be insignificant. Kosher salt has a slightly larger grain, so you'll want to use a teensy bit more than the recipes here call for if that is what you cook with.

FLAKY FINISHING SALT—I use a coarse-flaked Maldon sea salt as a finishing salt if I'm going for a more forward salty punch. I like to use this on fried eggs, spiced nuts, or the occasional grain salad that doesn't have a strong cheese involved.

OTHER PANTRY STAPLES

NUTS AND SEEDS—pistachios, walnuts, pepitas (pumpkin seeds), hazelnuts, Marcona and regular almonds (whole and slivered), pine nuts, sesame seeds, (white and black), quinoa.

GRAINS AND NOODLES—short-grain brown rice, jasmine rice, millet, bulgur, farro, whole wheat orzo, rice or quinoa pasta noodles, soba noodles, stone ground polenta, old-fashioned oats, steel-cut oats.

FLOURS: unbleached all-purpose, whole wheat pastry, spelt, oat, rye, buckwheat, rice, quinoa, cornmeal, almond meal.

ETC.—coconut milk, light coconut milk, sambal oelek (chili paste), Kalamata olives, low-sodium soy sauce, tamari, nut butters, lentils (red, French, and black Beluga); black, pinto, garbanzo, and white beans; jarred tomatoes, spices, vanilla and almond extracts.

MORNING BOWLS

I know breakfast looks incredibly different for everybody.
There are those who grab something portable on the way out,
others who need the quickest option as they have kids who
need tending, and then there are the few of us who truly look
forward to this meal to sit and savor first thing. Maybe you get
up early enough to make eggs before work, or a true breakfast
only happens on the weekends with coffee, orange juice, and
the newspaper. Either way, it's a time for a fresh start before
the day gets away from us.

    I prefer to start my morning with some protein, so you will
notice a number of egg dishes in this chapter. When I need
something quick, it's oats or granola; or when I'm running out
the door, I spread goat labneh or homemade ricotta on fresh-
cut whole grain bread to-go. I have found that starting the day
with real food sets a standard for the way I eat through the
rest of the day. A good breakfast sets the intention that I will
feed myself nutritious food throughout the day ahead of me.
A hot coffee and bowl of soft scrambled eggs are part of my
routine, baby on my hip or not, whether I have ten minutes
and eat standing or an hour to lounge in my sweatpants.
May your mornings be better with something delicious.

Baked Eggs *with* Barely Creamed Greens *and* Mustardy Bread Crumbs

Serves 4

This started as a *Bon Appétit* recipe that got repurposed for the blog, and now has made its way into bowl format for this book. I am always looking for everyday breakfasts that can be put together relatively quickly, especially with eggs. I bake these in small shallow baking dishes, but a large ramekin or cast-iron pan works great as well. I assume two eggs per person and serve it with fruit and toast for dipping into the yolks.

The French, who more beautifully call baked eggs *oeufs en cocotte*, often use a bain-marie for ideal egg texture, but I find the following approach just as suitable.

---

1 tablespoon coarse ground mustard

2 tablespoons Dijon mustard

1 tablespoon extra-virgin olive oil

¼ teaspoon sea salt

1½ cups fresh torn bread, in bite-size pieces

1 bunch Swiss chard (or spinach, kale, or a mix), stemmed and coarsely chopped (about 9 cups chopped)

1 tablespoon unsalted butter, plus more for the pans

1 shallot, minced

½ cup heavy cream or half-and-half

Fresh ground pepper

8 eggs, at room temperature

¾ cup grated Gruyére

Few sprigs of fresh thyme, for garnish

Chopped fresh parsley, for garnish

Preheat the oven to 400°F and set a rack in the upper third. Wipe the insides of four gratin dishes or large ramekins with butter and set on a baking sheet. In a small bowl, mix together the coarse ground mustard, 1 tablespoon of the Dijon mustard, the olive oil, and salt. Add the bread crumbs and toss to coat. Spread them on a baking sheet and bake for 10 to 12 minutes, until crispy. Set the bread crumbs aside, but leave the oven on.

In a large skillet over medium heat, add just enough water to cover the bottom; add the greens. Toss until wilted down, 2 to 3 minutes. Transfer to a strainer and press out the excess liquid. You should have about 2 heaping cups of greens. Wipe out the skillet and melt the butter over medium heat. Add the shallot and sauté until translucent, about 1 minute. Add the greens, the remaining tablespoon of Dijon mustard, the cream, and a pinch of salt and pepper. Stir until warmed through and just thickened, about 3 minutes.

Divide the greens between the prepared dishes and bake on the sheet in the upper third of the oven for 8 minutes. Remove sheet and carefully break two eggs onto the greens in each dish. Sprinkle the tops with a pinch of pepper and a few tablespoons of the Gruyére and bake for 6 minutes, until the whites are just cooked but the yolks are still runny. Let them sit for a minute to settle. Garnish with bread crumbs, thyme, and parsley.

Burrata *with* Figs *and* Crostini

There was a cafe by my old house that made wonderful breakfasts. Near the register, they kept a basket of small baguettes with a few different fillings for breakfast to-go. The flavors often changed, but the filling that always intrigued me was the fresh fig, fig preserves, and fresh mozzarella with balsamic glaze—perfect for a not-too-sweet breakfast. I've put that combination in a bowl, using mozzarella's cream-filled sister, burrata, which is slightly more decadent and getting easier to find in markets these days. While this bowl isn't something to take on the road, it makes a beautiful, light breakfast when figs are in season. Don't be fooled that this rests in the Morning Bowls chapter, it makes a great appetizer as well. Both the compote and the balsamic reduction can be made up to three days in advance.

I prefer dark-skinned figs here as they yield a pretty purple compote, but any variety will do. When they are ripe and in season, no added sugar is necessary. If your figs aren't that sweet, add a few tablespoons of natural cane sugar.

1 cup balsamic vinegar	1 French baguette
1 tablespoon honey	Extra-virgin olive oil, for brushing
Freshly ground pepper	Sea salt
1¼ pound figs, cleaned, halved or quartered depending on size	Fresh thyme, for garnish
⅓ cup apple juice	1 (5-ounce) ball burrata

In a pot over medium heat, add the balsamic vinegar and bring it to a boil. Turn it down to a quick simmer, and reduce the vinegar by half. Add the honey and a pinch of fresh black pepper and simmer until you have about ⅓ cup glaze. Note that it will thicken as it cools, so pull it off the heat once it reaches the viscosity of maple syrup. Transfer to a bowl and set aside.

Put ¾ pound of the figs and the apple juice in a pot and bring it to a simmer. Turn the heat to low and cook the figs down, stirring occasionally, until they fall apart and look like jam, about 1 hour.

Preheat the oven to 375°F. Slice the baguette ¼-inch thick on a very generous diagonal to get long crostini. Arrange them on a baking sheet, brush with a thin coat of olive oil, and sprinkle liberally with sea salt. Bake for 10 to 13 minutes until lightly toasted.

To serve, arrange a bowl with a big puddle of the compote, burrata, figs, a drizzle of the balsamic glaze and fresh thyme for garnish. Arrange the crostini on the side and assemble with a schmear of the compote, a slice of burrata, and a fresh fig on top.

Flourless Stone Fruit Breakfast Crumble

Serves 6

I'm tucking this into the breakfast chapter because it's a pretty virtuous crumble that could also pass as dessert with the right crowd. It's loads of lightly maple-sweetened fresh fruit and the crumble is gluten- and dairy-free, keeping your whole bowl tasting rather light. As dessert, I top it with coconut sorbet; but for a morning bowl, a hearty dollop of goat's milk yogurt is a repeat favorite.

You can find quinoa flakes online or at health food stores near the oats or whole grains. They are a great wheat-free, high-protein product that can be cooked into a breakfast cereal or adapted into some baked good recipes. If you cannot find them, give quick rolled oats a blitz in the food processor to get a very coarse-ground oat flour that works here as well. I spice this with vanilla, but if you are partial to cardamom, I really like a pinch of that in with the filling.

2½ pounds assorted stone fruit (nectarines, peaches, plums, cherries)

2 tablespoons orange juice

3 tablespoons coconut sugar or natural cane sugar

1 tablespoon cornstarch

1 vanilla bean, or ½ teaspoon pure vanilla extract

¼ teaspoon sea salt

—

CRUMBLE

1 cup quinoa flakes or coarse oat flour

1 cup almond meal

½ cup slivered almonds

1 teaspoon cinnamon

¼ teaspoon sea salt

⅓ cup maple syrup

⅓ cup coconut oil, just warmed to a liquid

1 teaspoon pure vanilla extract

Preheat the oven to 375°F.

Wash, pit, and slice the stone fruit into 1-inch wedges. Put them in a large mixing bowl, add the orange juice, coconut sugar, cornstarch, vanilla bean seeds, and salt and toss everything to mix.

For the crumble, in a large bowl, combine the quinoa, almond meal, almonds, cinnamon, and salt. Add the maple syrup, coconut oil, and vanilla and mix again.

Pour the fruit mixture into a 2½ quart baking dish or an 8-inch square pan and spread the crumble evenly on top, tucking some into the pockets. Shake the pan a little just to help everything settle. Bake on the middle rack for 30 minutes until the top is crisp and browned. Set aside to cool for at least 15 minutes and enjoy with yogurt or ice cream, as you wish.

Baby Potato *and* Asparagus Tangle *with* Green Harissa *and* Eggs

Serves 4

This green harissa has become a favorite around here; I add it to this bowl when I have a breakfast-for-dinner sort of evening. This is my go-to roasted potato method—a quick parboil, drain, season, and roast at high heat until crispy. Skip the egg part and you have a dinner side dish.

The roasty nubs of asparagus get tangled between the potatoes, creating a bed for your morning eggs. If you're one for bacon or crispy prosciutto, crumbled bits of it can be tossed in with the potato and asparagus.

The yolks, when poached or over easy, run into the potato-asparagus mixture and offer a subtle bit of moisture. For those who like to have extra sauce, the recipe will yield enough to serve more harissa on the side.

HARISSA

2 cloves garlic

1 cup parsley, plus more for garnish

½ cup cilantro

¼ cup mint leaves

1 serrano chile, stemmed and mostly seeded

Juice of ½ lemon

½ teaspoon cumin

½ teaspoon sea salt

—

⅓ cup extra-virgin olive oil

1½ pounds baby potatoes or Yukon golds, cut into 1-inch cubes

3 tablespoons extra-virgin olive oil

Sea salt

Freshly ground pepper

1 pound asparagus

1 cup packed arugula

4 to 8 eggs, depending on how hungry your guests are

¾ cup shaved pecorino or Parmesan

In a food processor, combine the garlic, parsley, cilantro, mint, serrano, lemon juice, cumin, salt and process to combine. With the motor running, drizzle in the olive oil until combined. Transfer to a jar and set aside.

Place a rack in the upper third of the oven and preheat to 425°F.

Put the potatoes in a pot and cover them with generously salted water by 2 inches. Bring the water to a boil and cook for about 5 minutes or until a knife just pierces through to the center. Drain completely and allow them to cool to the touch.

Spread the cooled potatoes on a rimmed baking sheet and toss with 2 tablespoons of the olive oil, salt, and a few grinds of black pepper. Place the tray in the upper third of the oven and roast for 30 to 35 minutes until crispy.

While the potatoes cook, chop the asparagus into 2-inch nubs on a diagonal. Toss them with the remaining tablespoon of olive oil and a pinch of salt and pepper. Spread them on a baking sheet and roast for 15 minutes, until the edges begin to brown. When the potatoes are done, combine the asparagus and potatoes and toss them in two hearty spoonfuls of the harissa to coat. Add the arugula and toss again, adding more harissa if you wish.

Poach the eggs, one or two per person, for about 3 minutes (or however you like your eggs).

Serve each bowl with a portion of the potatoes, top with an egg or two and a generous sprinkle of pecorino and chopped parsley.

Mushroom *and* Leek Soft Egg Bake

Serves 4 to 6

I will choose eggs for breakfast six days out of seven (one day is for waffles or pancakes). Most of the time I scramble them for the sake of lots of vegetable mix-ins, I poach on occasion for aesthetics, and otherwise I do a thin, individual frittata in my smallest skillet and pop it in the toaster oven to melt a little cheese on top. To serve more than two people, a frittata, or egg bake, is generally the answer and I aim to keep these eggs tender with a little cream and a lower-than-standard temperature. I'm going for the sort of egg bake you would eat from a bowl with some delicate, dressed greens on top, not a firm, pie-sliced shape of tough eggs. Serve this bowl with a piece of toasty fresh bread.

---

3 cups (16 ounces) mushrooms	1 tablespoon hot sauce
2 tablespoons unsalted butter	Freshly ground pepper
2 leeks, cleaned, halved lengthwise, and thinly sliced	4 ounces soft goat cheese (chèvre)
Sea salt	Baby arugula, for garnish
9 eggs	Olive oil, for dressing
¼ cup chopped flat-leaf parsley	Freshly squeezed lemon juice, for dressing
⅓ cup heavy cream or whole milk	

Place the rack in the middle of the oven and preheat the oven to 325°F.

Wipe the mushrooms clean with a damp paper towel, remove the stems, and thinly slice. Heat a large skillet over medium heat. Add the mushrooms and a few pinches of salt to the dry pan and cook, stirring occasionally, until they release most of their liquid, about 10 minutes. Add 1 tablespoon of the butter and sauté until the edges brown a bit. Transfer to a bowl and set aside. Warm the remaining tablespoon of butter in the skillet. Add the leeks to the pan with a pinch of salt and sauté until they begin to brown, about 8 minutes. Transfer them to the bowl with the mushrooms.

In another mixing bowl, whisk the eggs, parsley, heavy cream, hot sauce, and another hearty pinch of salt and pepper until very well mixed. Stir in the mushrooms and leeks. Grease a 2-quart baking dish. Pour the eggs into the dish and crumble the goat cheese on top. Bake the eggs for 40 to 45 minutes until mostly set with the center still a bit jiggly; it will look underdone, but trust me, it will set as it rests. Let cool for 5 to 10 minutes.

Lightly dress the arugula with a drizzle of olive oil, lemon juice, and a pinch of salt and pepper. Scoop the eggs into a bowl, top with the arugula, and serve with toast.

Goat Labneh

Makes 1 cup

A few years ago, I started to pledge allegiance to the claim that goat dairy is easier to digest than cow dairy, and tried to substitute the former as much as I could. It does not contain nearly the amount of lactose as cow dairy and the protein structure is completely different, making it much gentler on our insides to process. You can do your research, but either way, this labneh is delicious. I include a few of my favorite ideas below, but think of it as the more familiar Greek yogurt—rich, spreadable, versatile enough to go between sweet and savory.

This recipe yields a moderate amount, in case you're not certain how often you'll use it, but the yield is easily doubled—you simply need a bigger strainer and bowl to collect the liquid.

2 cups plain goat yogurt	Pinch of sea salt

Double line a strainer with cheesecloth and set it over a large, deep bowl. Stir the salt into the yogurt and pour the yogurt into the cheesecloth. Tie the ends of the cheesecloth together to make a secure bundle. Stick a wooden spoon through the knot of the bundle, making sure it's double knotted, and suspend the yogurt bundle over the bowl. You don't want the bundle to touch the liquid at the bottom; tie the knot up tighter or get a deeper bowl if necessary. Refrigerate overnight or for 10 hours—less if you like it softer, longer it you prefer it on the thicker side. Transfer the labneh to a container and store covered in the fridge for up to 1 week.

SERVING SUGGESTIONS:

- as a dip with toasted pita chips, drizzled with good quality extra-virgin olive oil, a few sprigs of fresh thyme, and za'atar

- on toast with blackberry jam or fresh figs

- as a spread for a wrap with sprouts and shredded raw beets, carrots, and cucumbers

- as a spread for a crisp waffle with fresh berries on top

- with granola and fresh fruit

the sprouted kitchen bowl + spoon

Pumpkin Pie Steel-Cut Oats

While not the most gorgeous bowl on the block, this spiced bowl of warm, orange-hued oats is a nice change from my traditional choice of plain oats with maple syrup and berries. The pureed pumpkin makes the oats almost meaty, for lack of better description, and a filling start to your day. I use a 4-quart pot so the oats have plenty of space to cook evenly; I also find this gives me less scorching on the bottom.

Adjust the spices to your preference; I use pretty moderate amounts. You could add up to 1½ teaspoons of a pumpkin pie spice blend if you have one you like. When I have some on hand, I sprinkle a little granola on top for crunch and to really complete the pumpkin pie experience.

---

1 tablespoon unsalted butter	¾ teaspoon cinnamon
1 cup steel cut-oats	¼ teaspoon freshly ground nutmeg
3 cups water	½ teaspoon ground ginger
1 cup milk or non-dairy milk of choice	—
½ teaspoon sea salt	4 tablespoons maple syrup
⅓ cup pumpkin puree	1 cup toasted pecan pieces
2 tablespoons muscovado or brown sugar	

In a large, heavy pot or saucepan, melt the butter. Add the oats and sauté until fragrant, about 5 minutes. Remove oats and set aside.

Back in the pot, bring the water, milk, and salt to a simmer. Slowly stir in the oats, keeping the heat on a gentle simmer. Cook, stirring occasionally to keep the bottom from scorching, for 25 minutes, or until the mixture is soft and loose. Stir in the pumpkin, sugar, cinnamon, nutmeg, and ginger and cook another few minutes for the flavors to blend.

The oats will thicken as they rest. Serve each bowl with a drizzle of maple syrup and chopped pecans.

Popeye Protein Bowl

I try to eat well consistently to avoid getting sucked into extreme cleansing or diet trends, but seasons of indulgence make their way in with holidays, celebrations, and the like. After heavier fare gets the best of me, I prefer to keep breakfast super light so I stay inspired to eat clean throughout the day—if I start healthy, the day follows suit.

The texture of scrambled egg whites is pretty dry. I try to help their case with a little milk and lower heat, but the texture is just something to expect—use whole eggs if you prefer. You can use canned beans here or cook them from scratch; either way I like to keep them warm in broth for a little more flavor. If I need more with this meal, I'll fire up a brown rice tortilla over the stove and use it to scoop up the eggs. A dollop of sour cream and hot sauce or some goat cheese to top things off is excellent as well.

2 cups cooked black beans

1 cup vegetable broth

2 cups arugula

3 teaspoons extra-virgin olive oil

Juice of ¼ lemon

Sea salt and freshly ground pepper

1 zucchini, diced

2 cups baby spinach

3 green onions, white and green parts, sliced

6 egg whites

2 tablespoons whole milk or nondairy milk

1 large avocado, sliced

Chopped fresh chives, for topping

Salsa, for topping (optional)

Sour cream, for topping (optional)

In a small pot over low heat, combine the beans and broth. Cover and warm through.

In another bowl, dress the arugula with 1 teaspoon of the olive oil, a small squeeze of lemon juice, and a pinch of salt and pepper and set aside.

In a non-stick skillet over medium heat, warm the remaining olive oil. Add the zucchini and cook for 5 to 7 minutes, until it softens and begins to brown. Add the green onions and baby spinach and sauté another minute to warm through. Put the egg whites and milk in a bowl, add a pinch of salt and pepper and whisk well. Turn the heat to low, add the egg mixture to the vegetable skillet, and cook, stirring occasionally, until just firm, 2 to 3 minutes.

Assemble your bowl with a scoop of the beans, a helping of the scramble, and top with avocado, chives, and some dressed arugula. Serve with salsa and sour cream, if you wish.

Cabbage, Fennel, *and* Apple Slaw *with* Smoked Salmon Toasts

Serves 4

A great brunch spot near us serves a starter of rye toast points with crème fraîche, smoked salmon, and thinly sliced apples. It is so simply delightful—a perfect combination. I figured there's no reason not to repurpose it in bowl form. You could even arrange this combination atop crostini for an appetizer and enjoy it as part of a larger brunch spread.

The trick to the slaw is getting the ingredients sliced thin. A mandoline works best, but careful knife skills will do. I pass no judgment on buying preshredded cabbage, the thinner the better.

Smoked salmon, gravlax, and lox are different. What I like best for this bowl is a cold smoked salmon, which is tender and typically sold very thinly sliced. A hot smoked salmon will have a tougher texture and flakes apart in larger chunks instead of delicate slices. This is a brunch item at our house, but if you're serving it for lunch or dinner, a piece of poached or grilled salmon also dishes up well with the slaw.

---

1 small head (12 ounces) green cabbage, finely shredded

1 large fennel bulb

1 green apple

⅓ cup coarsely chopped fresh dill, plus more for garnish

¼ cup grapeseed oil or other high-heat oil

—

DRESSING

1 shallot, minced (about 2 tablespoons)

3 tablespoons white wine vinegar

1 teaspoon honey

1 teaspoon Dijon mustard

¼ cup crème fraîche

¼ cup extra-virgin olive oil or grapeseed oil

¼ teaspoon sea salt

½ teaspoon freshly ground pepper

¼ cup capers, drained and dried

¼ cup cornstarch

⅓ cup crème fraîche

2 ounces soft goat cheese (chèvre)

2 tablespoons fresh chopped chives, plus more for garnish

Freshly ground pepper

4 slices rye bread, toasted and halved

16 ounces smoked salmon

Put the shredded cabbage in a large mixing bowl. Cut the fennel in half, remove the core, and slice it very thin. Cut the apple in half lengthwise, cut out the core, and slice it very thin or cut into matchsticks. You can also use a mandoline or the shredder blade on a food processor for slicing. Add the fennel, apples, and dill to the mixing bowl.

For the dressing, put the minced shallot in a bowl. Add the vinegar, honey, mustard, and crème fraîche and whisk to blend. Whisk in the olive oil, salt, and pepper. Adjust seasoning to taste. Dress the slaw and allow it to sit for a few minutes.

In a small skillet, heat the grapeseed oil over medium-high heat. In a fine mesh sieve, toss the dried capers in the cornstarch to coat, shaking off the excess cornstarch. Fry the capers in the hot oil, only stirring them once or twice, until crispy, about 2 minutes. Transfer them with a slotted spoon to a paper towel-lined plate.

Mix the crème fraîche, goat cheese, chives, and pepper together until smooth. Spread it on the toasted bread, top with a slice of smoked salmon, and sprinkle a few more chives and fresh pepper on top.

Arrange four bowls with a portion of the slaw, salmon toasts, and a sprinkle of crispy capers. Garnish with fresh dill.

Homemade Ricotta

Makes about 2 cups

(slightly less for the goat's milk ricotta)

When I first became interested in cooking, I watched my fair share of the Food Network. I saw Ina Garten make ricotta one day and realized how easy it is to make at home. The result is a creamy, fresh cheese that trumps the supermarket version by a long shot. I took her ratio and brought the amount of cream down, which then led to trials with goat milk. I am including both options here and they follow the same process. For the goat milk version, the ricotta curdles a bit less. If you can find fresh or even pasteurized instead of ultra-pasteurized goat milk, it will turn out better.

I like to serve the ricotta in a bowl with a little honey, some halved fresh cherries, and a handful of Seedy Olive Oil Granola (page 24).

COW MILK RICOTTA	GOAT MILK RICOTTA
4 cups whole milk	4 cups goat milk, preferably not ultra-pasteurized
1⅓ cups heavy cream	4 tablespoons lemon juice
2 tablespoons lemon juice	1 teaspoon sea salt
1 tablespoon apple cider or white wine vinegar	
1 teaspoon sea salt	

For cow milk ricotta, in a large nonreactive pot, combine the milk and cream and heat to a simmer. Turn off the heat and very gently stir in the lemon juice and vinegar. You only need a quick, gentle stir to distribute the vinegar; stirring too much will break the curds. Let the curds and whey separate, undisturbed, for 5 to 8 minutes.

For goat milk ricotta, follow this same process but replace the milk and cream with the goat milk and add only the 4 tablespoons of lemon juice, no vinegar; then follow the rest of the recipe.

Set a mesh strainer on top of a deep bowl and line the strainer with the cheesecloth. Carefully pour the curds and whey into the prepared strainer. Allow the liquid to drain. You can gently pull the cheesecloth back and forth to expedite the process and make more room. Allow the ricotta to drain for 25 to 45 minutes, depending on how thick you prefer it. It will firm up a bit more in the fridge. Stir in the salt and store, refrigerated, in a covered container.

Ricotta will keep for about 1 week.

Seedy Olive Oil Granola

Makes about 6 cups

One day, in an attempt not to waste a nearly stale box of brown rice crisp cereal, I threw some into the dry mix of our weekly batch of granola. This may not be for everyone and perhaps it's some sort of granola blasphemy, but now I don't make a batch without it. It changes up the texture, giving you crispier bits between the shattering oats. I use olive oil here, but a scant ½ cup of melted coconut oil works great as well. Play around with the spices and seeds of choice, but keep the ratio of liquid sweetener to fat to dry ingredients.

You'll also notice this version doesn't include dried fruit. My typical preparation is a big bowl of berries, almond milk, and a scoop of this granola. I find that adding fresh fruit is just the sweetness I want; adding dried fruit ends up being too much. If your granola is more for snacking, stir in your dried fruit of choice after baking—apricots, cherries, or currants would be nice.

½ cup extra-virgin olive oil

⅔ cup pure maple syrup

¾ teaspoon sea salt

½ teaspoon cardamom

1 teaspoon cinnamon

3½ cups old-fashioned oats

2 cups crisp rice cereal

½ cup raw pepitas (pumpkin seeds)

1 cup raw sunflower seeds

3 tablespoons chia, hemp, sesame, flax seeds, or a mixture

Place the rack in the middle of the oven and preheat to 325°F.

Mix the olive oil, maple syrup, sea salt, cardamom, and cinnamon in a large mixing bowl. Add the oats, crisp rice, pepitas, sunflower seeds, and chia seeds. Mix to coat.

Spread the granola mixture on a large rimmed baking sheet in a single layer. Use 2 sheets if it looks crowded. Bake on for 40 to 45 minutes or until the mixture is toasty, stirring every 15 minutes to ensure even crispness. Set aside to cool completely.

Granola will keep in an airtight container for 2 weeks.

Winter Fruit Salad in Ginger Lime Syrup

Serves 6

Fruit salad in the summer is too easy. The winter option, while the fruit bounty pulls back, is more limited but still possible. The syrup can be made a day in advance, kept covered in the fridge, and poured on top just before serving. The sauce is thin, as I don't like a sticky, thick coat on fresh fruit; so when dressing, start moderately and drizzle to taste. I add the hemp seeds on top without tossing them in to preserve texture, but you could go without them as well.

The citrus can be segmented in advance, but the persimmon and pears start to weather with time, so cut those and add just before serving.

1 grapefruit	**SYRUP**
2 blood oranges	¼ cup maple syrup, grade A
3 clementines	1 tablespoon water
1 persimmon	3-inch piece of fresh ginger, peeled and sliced
1 red pear	2 tablespoons freshly squeezed lime juice
1 Asian pear	—
1 pomegranate (about 1 cup seeds)	1 to 2 tablespoons finely chopped fresh mint
—	Hemp seeds, for garnish (optional)

To segment, or supreme, the citrus, trim off the top and bottom of each fruit, cut off all the skin and pith, and then use a sharp paring knife to slice between the membranes to remove each wedge of the flesh. Put the segments in a large mixing bowl with any remaining juices. Slice thinly the persimmon and red and Asian pears and add them to the bowl. Seed the pomegranate and reserve the seeds.

To make the syrup, put the maple syrup and water in a small saucepan over medium heat. Add the ginger, bring it up to a simmer, turn off the heat and let the ginger steep for at least 15 minutes. Stir in the lime juice, remove the ginger pieces, and pour the cooled syrup over the fruit. Gently toss to coat. Garnish with hemp seeds, mint, and pomegranate seeds.

Golden Quinoa *and* Butternut Breakfast Bowl

Serves 4

My favorite breakfast spot in Los Angeles is Huckleberry Bakery. They have a glistening pastry case filled with rustic baked goods and treats of all kinds and a big chalkboard that lists a very fresh, yet somehow decadent, menu. I will never forget the first breakfast I enjoyed there and how impressed I was with their savory breakfast bowl. This is how I recreate it at home, simplified from theirs, but still a beautiful bowl for chilly fall mornings. I use quinoa, but any cooked grain will work—try bulgur, spelt, millet, barley, and the like. The style of eggs on top is up to you. I love the nuttiness of Manchego, but Parmesan works too, either way be generous with the cheese.

HERB OIL

2 tablespoons chopped fresh parsley

2 tablespoons chopped fresh chives

⅓ cup extra-virgin olive oil

2 teaspoons fresh lemon zest

Sea salt and pepper

—

1 small butternut squash (1½ pounds), peeled, seeded, and cut into ½-inch cubes

2½ tablespoons extra-virgin olive oil or coconut oil

¼ teaspoon cinnamon

¼ teaspoon freshly grated nutmeg

Sea salt and freshly ground pepper

2 cloves garlic, minced

¼ of a yellow onion, finely diced

3 cups coarsely chopped baby kale

2 cups cooked quinoa

1 tablespoon maple syrup

Pinch of cayenne pepper, to taste

Juice of ½ lemon

8 eggs

1 cup shaved Manchego cheese

For the herb oil, in a food processor or high-powered blender, blitz the parsley, chives, olive oil, lemon zest, and a pinch of salt until mostly smooth. Set aside.

Position rack to the upper third of the oven and preheat to 425°F. Spread the squash cubes on a large rimmed baking sheet. Drizzle with 1 tablespoon of the olive oil, cinnamon, nutmeg, and a few pinches of salt and pepper. Toss to coat and spread in a single layer. Bake for 20 to 25 minutes until the edges are browned and caramelized. Remove to cool slightly.

In a large frying pan over medium heat, heat the remaining 1½ tablespoons of oil until shimmering. Add the garlic, onion, and a pinch of salt and sauté for 1 minute. Add the kale, quinoa, maple syrup, and cayenne and sauté until the quinoa starts to get crispy, 6 to 8 minutes. Transfer the quinoa mixture to a bowl and stir in 1 tablespoon of the herb oil, the squash, and lemon juice.

Serve each bowl with a scoop of quinoa, eggs of your choice, a drizzle of herb oil, and shaved cheese.

Tropical Smoothie Bowl

Serves 4

I add turmeric here for all its fabulous health benefits, and its color blends right in so the skeptics don't turn up their noses. The discerning may get a hint of the flavor, but it's very subtle and worth adding. If you are partial, you could add even more. You want the smoothie on the thicker side. A thick texture makes it more appropriate to eat from a bowl and spoon, almost like frozen yogurt with all its goodies on top.

2 cups frozen mango

1 cup frozen pineapple

½ cup coconut water

½ cup orange juice

¾ cup coconut milk

1 teaspoon turmeric (optional)

2 bananas

1 to 2 tablespoons bee pollen (optional)

1 cup crisped rice cereal

¾ cup toasted coconut flakes

¾ cup toasted, chopped macadamia nuts

Blend the mango, pineapple, coconut water, orange juice, coconut milk, and turmeric until very smooth. Distribute evenly among four bowls. Cut the banana into thin slices. Garnish each bowl with portions of banana slices, bee pollen, crisp rice cereal, coconut flakes, and macadamia nuts.

Soaked Oat Porridge

Serves 4

You can dress up this humble bowl any which way—with maple syrup, milk, or fruit—but one tip worth passing on is the mix of textures. Chef April Bloomfield shared that idea in her last book and I think it's simply brilliant. Steel-cut oats give the dish texture and chewy bits, while the rolled oats melt between the steel-cut, making a warm bowl of oats just a bit more interesting. I soak the steel-cut oats overnight to cut down on the cooking time, and also because the soaking of any legume or grain makes them easier to digest. If you skip this step, simply add 15 minutes to the cooking time in the morning. I prefer my oats very loose; you can alter the liquid ratio to your preference.

I opt for fresh fruit over dried, but if you don't have any, dried raisins, cherries, or apricots will stand in just fine. I sweeten with a bit of maple syrup and a dollop of crème fraîche for optimum creaminess. You can use coconut cream instead of crème fraîche, just refrigerate a can of full-fat coconut milk overnight. Once the can is chilled, gently spoon a dollop of the cream off the top. Just trust me on this last step.

---

1 cup steel-cut oats	½ teaspoon pure vanilla extract
2 cups nondairy or dairy milk of choice	Maple syrup, for serving
2 cups water	Crème fraîche or coconut cream, for serving
1 cup rolled rye or wheat oats, or a blend of these	2 cups sliced strawberries, peaches, or mixed berries
Pinch of salt	

The night before you make the oats, in a bowl, combine the steel-cut oats with water to cover by 2 inches; cover and let sit overnight.

In the morning, drain the oats. Warm the milk and water in a medium pot, add the steel-cut oats, rolled oats, a pinch of salt, and vanilla extract. Gently simmer the grains for 10 to 15 minutes until warmed and thickened, adding more liquid if needed for the desired consistency.

Serve the warm grains in a bowl with a spoonful or two of maple syrup, crème fraîche or coconut cream, and top with the fruit.

SIDE BOWLS

For the omnivore, sides are what complete a meal—the bright acidity in a salad or creamy starch that pairs well with your protein. Or for some of us, large portions of sides are our meal or, at the very least, a passable lunch. I consider these bowls a side for company, but many of them are great dishes to pack for a picnic or work. I make a bowl of the **Kale Slaw with Soaked Golden Raisins *and* Pine Nuts** (page 41) or **Marrakesh Carrots** (page 61) for travel as they keep well, or a batch of the **Spiced Sweet Potato Chips** (page 77) when my nieces are over and I want a special snack. A lot of these bowls are the workhorses of weekday lunches in our house—dishes I keep in the fridge so anyone can grab something when they're hungry. Big bowls of whole grains, colorful produce, and a snappy dressing are the reason I got hooked on "bowl foods" in the first place.

Please trust yourself in seasoning these bowls; you, the cook, can leave out the cheese, add more spice, anything that makes them work for the way you like to eat.

California Quinoa

There is a handful of produce that I associate with California—avocados, citrus, perfect strawberries, late summer figs. Of the less mainstream sort, things like plump pomegranates, persimmons, and fragrant fennel fill fall menus with their intriguing colors and textures. This is the easy-to-throw-together quinoa salad that works along with the rest of your dinner plans. The flavors are pretty neutral, good for appreciating the produce at its peak. If you can't find a persimmon, an apple or pear will work. The cheese here is up for discussion. I add goat cheese because it's my favorite, but something like a shaved Parmesan or crumbled feta will also work well. Toss the cheese in just before serving to preserve its texture. This is my favorite sort of salad to keep on hand to pack for lunch; I just add some leftover grilled salmon, roasted tofu, or another protein to fill it out.

¾ cup quinoa

1½ cups vegetable broth

1 small fennel bulb

1 Fuyu persimmon

3 green onions, white and green parts

½ cup pomegranate seeds

½ cup cooked lentils (preferably French green or black)

⅓ cup coarsely chopped cilantro

2 tablespoons extra-virgin olive oil

2 tablespoons white wine vinegar

½ cup crumbled goat cheese (about 4 ounces)

½ cup toasted pistachios, coarsely chopped

Sea salt and freshly ground pepper

Rinse the quinoa in a fine mesh strainer. Put it in a pot with the broth. Bring it up to a boil, then down to a gentle simmer; cover and cook for 13 to 15 minutes. Fluff it with a fork, turn off the heat, leave the cover ajar, and allow it to cool completely.

Cut the fennel in half lengthwise and very thinly slice, using a mandoline if you have one. Do the same with the persimmon. Finely chop the green onions. Collect everything in a large mixing bowl and add the pomegranate seeds, lentils, and cilantro. Add the oil, vinegar, and a few hearty pinches each of salt and pepper. Add the cooled quinoa, and toss everything to coat. Adjust seasoning to taste. Top the salad with the crumbled goat cheese and chopped pistachios and serve.

Kale Slaw *with* Soaked Golden Raisins *and* Pine Nuts

Serves 4

I am always experimenting with green salads that work for potluck dinners or can sit in the fridge to have on hand for quick lunches. The sturdy kale can hold up dressed in the fridge for an extra day or two, so I make a large bowl and repurpose it with added beans or protein. This is a salad so light it is nearly effortless to eat, with its thin shreds of kale, a blend of sweet and tart raisins, and salty flecks of cheese.

Your bunch of kale and mine will differ in size. If you would like your greens more dressed, simply drizzle in a bit more olive oil and vinegar.

½ cup golden raisins

⅓ cup plus 2 tablespoons white balsamic vinegar

1 bunch lacinato kale (5 to 6 cups chopped)

3 tablespoons extra-virgin olive oil

Sea salt and freshly ground pepper

¼ teaspoon red pepper flakes

⅓ cup toasted pine nuts

1 shallot, finely minced

Pecorino, to taste

Combine the raisins, ⅓ cup of the vinegar, and 2 tablespoons of hot water in a small dish. Set aside for at least 15 minutes. If you want a more acidulated flavor, let the raisins sit overnight.

Remove the stems from the kale and chop the leaves well—you want small pieces, like something you could eat with a spoon. Transfer to a large bowl and drizzle on the remaining vinegar, olive oil, a generous pinch of salt and pepper, and the red pepper flakes. Toss with your hands to dress rubbing the dressing into the kale to soften and let it sit for 10 minutes to absorb some of the dressing.

Drain the liquid from the raisins and add them to the kale with the pine nuts, shallot, and pecorino to taste. Give the salad one more toss and serve.

Snap Pea *and* Edamame Salad

Serves 4

This is intended to be a very light side salad—something you would serve alongside a dish you don't want to compete with. A lot of the salads I make are written to stand alone or dress up for company with some protein added. This is a side dish, and the salad I make anytime we have the Ahi Poke Bowls (page 91) or other Asian-seasoned proteins. If you don't come across black sesame seeds, two tablespoons of white sesame will be just fine. You can add some roasted tofu and toasted cashews to make this a meal.

---

1 pound sugar snap peas, trimmed and thinly sliced on the diagonal

¾ cup steamed, shelled edamame beans

3 cups thinly sliced cabbage

2 to 3 green onions, white and light green parts, thinly sliced

¼ cup chopped cilantro

2 tablespoons chopped mint

1 tablespoon toasted black sesame seeds

1 tablespoon toasted white sesame seeds

—

DRESSING

2 teaspoons yellow miso

1 teaspoon honey

2 tablespoons toasted sesame oil

2 tablespoons rice wine vinegar

Juice of 1 lime

Pinch of red pepper flakes

Sea salt and freshly ground pepper

1 tablespoon each black sesame seeds and toasted white sesame seeds

---

Add the peas to a large bowl with the edamame, cabbage, green onions, cilantro, and mint. Stir everything together.

For the dressing, in another bowl, whisk together the miso, honey, sesame oil, rice vinegar, lime juice, red pepper flakes, and pinch of salt and pepper until smooth. Pour the dressing over the vegetables and toss to coat. Sprinkle on both sesame seeds and chill the salad until ready to serve.

Chunky Mediterranean Eggplant Dip

Serves 4

This is a riff on my two favorite Middle Eastern dips—hummus and baba ghanoush. If I'm thinking ahead for this dip, I grill extra eggplant slices while the grill is hot. Otherwise, you may prick a few holes in the eggplant and either broil the whole thing in the oven until it collapses or char the entire eggplant over a flame on the stove (messy, but effective). After cooling, most of the skin should peel off easily, and leaving a little intact for the dip is fine. If you do char it whole, the strip of seeds should be easy to pull out from the center after cooking, so remove those.

Pomegranate molasses can be found online, at health food stores, or in the international section of larger markets. It adds an intriguing depth of flavor, but the dip can be made using a dark honey as an alternative.

1 clove garlic	2 tablespoons tahini
1 small shallot	1 tablespoon pomegranate molasses
½ teaspoon sea salt	2 cups cooked (or one 15-ounce can) garbanzo beans, well drained
1 teaspoon freshly ground pepper	
1½ teaspoons za'atar, plus more for garnish	1 large eggplant (about 1 pound), charred and coarsely chopped
1 tablespoon red wine vinegar	¼ cup coarsely chopped flat-leaf parsley
2 tablespoons extra-virgin olive oil	¼ cup coarsely chopped cilantro
	2 tablespoons chopped mint leaves

In a food processor, combine the garlic, shallot, salt, pepper, za'atar, vinegar, oil, tahini, and pomegranate molasses and pulse to combine. Add the beans, eggplant, and herbs and give the mixture 3 to 5 pulses, just to combine. A little texture here is welcome.

Transfer the dip to a bowl, sprinkle with a bit more za'atar, and serve with warm pita bread or chips.

The dip will keep, covered, in the fridge for 1 week.

Chickpea Deli Salad

The lunch I pack for a long beach day typically includes a light tuna salad, specifically the one in our last cookbook. Turns out I am the only one in the family who likes tuna, so I've moved on to a deli-style salad of chickpeas. It is barely creamy, bright with lemon and herbs, crunchy with celery, and has just a hint of sweetness from being dotted with golden raisins. I eat this on a pile of greens with a side of crackers or stuff it in a pita with some crumbled feta as a portable and, dare I say, kid-friendly alternative.

I find freshly cooked beans have a sturdier texture, but canned will work here if you're short on time. If that's the case, I'd suggest peeling the skins off the beans (mind numbing, I know, just go for the majority, not every single bean) for a cleaner texture in the end. If mayonnaise or the vegan alternative doesn't sit well with you, extra-virgin olive oil will work in its place.

---

2 tablespoons veganaise or good-quality mayonnaise

3 tablespoons freshly squeezed lemon juice

Sea salt and freshly ground pepper

2 to 3 celery stalks, finely diced

¼ cup minced red onion

⅓ cup golden raisins

2 cups cooked chickpeas (or roughly one 15-ounce can, rinsed and drained)

¼ cup chopped flat-leaf parsley

1 tablespoon chopped chives

In a large bowl, whisk together the veganaise, lemon juice, and a few pinches of salt and pepper.

Add the celery, red onion, and raisins to the dressing. Give the chickpeas a coarse chop and add them to the bowl along with the parsley and chives. Stir every-thing to mix well. Taste for salt and pepper and adjust as desired. Chill for at least 30 minutes for the flavors to blend. Salad will keep in the refregirator for one week.

Emerald Greens

Serves 6

It took time and practice on our blog to figure out a fluid way to write recipes. When I look back in the archives at some of my first ones, I can't even follow what I am saying, though the good intentions are still there. This recipe was one of the first, and I have improved it slightly here (if mostly just by sensible directions). I still find the uncomplicated combination of broccoli and leeks with a little bit of time in the oven the most lovely, simple side dish. Cooking with fresh produce makes for naturally gorgeous food, and all the monochromatic greens here look fabulous together. I find romanesco at my farmers market, but cauliflower could work as well.

This dish is great served warm or cold. It can be tossed with some of your favorite cooked grains or goes well with pretty much any protein.

---

2 pounds broccoli

1 pound romanesco or broccolini

2 leeks

5 tablespoons extra-virgin olive oil

Zest of 2 small lemons

3 cloves garlic, minced

1 teaspoon each sea salt and ground pepper

3 cups baby spinach, coarsely chopped

Juice of 2 small lemons

Pinch of red pepper flakes

⅓ cup chopped flat-leaf parsley

½ cup slivered almonds, or ⅓ cup pine nuts, toasted

1 cup crumbled, good-quality feta cheese

Place the racks in the upper and lower thirds of the oven and preheat to 425°F.

Discard the lower stem of the broccoli, leaving about 2 inches intact. Cut the broccoli and romanesco into 2-inch pieces; stems may be included but discard the larger, tough parts. Clean and halve the leeks lengthwise, slice into half circles. In a large mixing bowl, combine the broccoli, romanesco, and the leeks. Drizzle with 3 tablespoons of the olive oil, and add the lemon zest, garlic, sea salt, and pepper and toss to coat.

Spread the vegetables on 2 large rimmed baking sheets and roast for 20 to 22 minutes, rotating them halfway, until just starting to brown on top.

Put the baby spinach in the mixing bowl. When you remove the hot vegetables, pour them on top of the spinach along with the remaining 2 tablespoons of the olive oil, lemon juice, and pepper flakes and toss to barely wilt. Add the parsley and almonds and toss again. Top with the crumbled feta.

This salad can be served warm or chilled.

Grapefruit *and* Shaved Fennel Salad

Serves 4

I love huge, hearty bowls of salad, but this is more delicate, one you would have as a starter course or something you could put out for a brunch. The greens get tangled with the fennel and the grapefruit segments offer a sweet and tart bite, perfect to begin a meal or complement another dish. Grapefruit and fennel both go along excellently with seafood dishes—either white fish or a big salmon fillet are my preferences. You can find sweet and juicy grapefruit in the winter and spring, and while available year-round, I find they can get too tart off-season.

The dressing is simple. I season it generously, as the ingredients have strong flavors and need it. If you'd like a little more decadence, and to temper the tartness, add a dollop of crème fraîche. While not crucial, it's a perfect addition.

---

2 tablespoons extra-virgin olive oil

2 tablespoons white wine vinegar

2 teaspoon maple syrup

¼ teaspoon sea salt

¼ teaspoon freshly ground pepper

—

1 red grapefruit, skin and pith removed

1 small fennel bulb

3 spears (about 4 ounces) hearts of palm, cut into ½-inch diagonal slices

2 tablespoons chopped fresh mint leaves

1 cup watercress

2 cups mixed baby greens

1 cup microgreens

1 tablespoon black sesame seeds (optional)

In a small bowl, whisk together the olive oil, vinegar, maple syrup, salt, and pepper.

To segment, or supreme, the grapefruit, trim off the top and bottom, cut off all the skin and pith, and then use a sharp paring knife to slice between the membranes to remove each wedge of the flesh. Transfer the grapefruit to a mixing bowl along with any excess juice. Shave the fennel extra thin, with a mandoline or careful knife skills, and add the fennel, hearts of palm, mint, watercress, baby greens, and microgreens to the mixing bowl. Drizzle with the dressing and toss to coat. Sprinkle with the seeds and serve immediately.

Harvest-Roasted Delicata Squash

Serves 4

I mourn summer's exit as the tomatoes, corn, and peaches leave the markets, but fall squash makes me quickly forget what I'm missing. Butternut, kabocha, acorn . . . all easy to find and excellent roasted. Delicata squash are a little trickier to get your hands on and their window of availability slightly shorter, at least near me, but they are my favorite of the group. First off, you can eat the thin skin, which makes prep easy. They have a subtle corn and sweet potato flavor that marries sweetness and spice just beautifully. I layer the flavors of maple, soy sauce, nutritional yeast, and cayenne so they all come through but none take over. The amount of cayenne here will give you just enough heat without being spicy, making it a great side dish for autumn dinners.

2½ pounds delicata squash (about 3 small squash)

2½ tablespoons extra-virgin olive oil

1 tablespoon maple syrup

2 teaspoons soy sauce

2 teaspoons nutritional yeast (optional)

¼ teaspoon cayenne

1 small bunch Swiss chard

1 tablespoon apple cider vinegar

Sea salt and pepper

½ cup toasted hazelnuts, chopped

Preheat the oven to 375°F and position rack to upper third. Line a large rimmed baking sheet with parchment or foil. Cut the squash in half lengthwise and scoop out the seeds. Slice the squash into ¾-inch half circles. In a small bowl, mix together 1½ tablespoons of the olive oil, the maple syrup, soy sauce, nutritional yeast, and cayenne. Pile the squash on a large rimmed baking sheet, pouring the dressing on top, and toss everything to coat. Spread the squash in an even layer, avoiding overlap. Roast the squash for 35 to 40 minutes, until the edges are browned.

Meanwhile, remove the thick ribs and stems from the chard. Chop the leaves finely (you should have about 2 cups) and add them to a large mixing bowl. Drizzle the remaining olive oil, apple cider vinegar, a generous pinch of salt and pepper, and toss everything to coat. Add the squash, while still warm, to the chard and toss to combine. The squash will gently warm up the chard, still leaving it pretty crisp. Season to taste with salt and paper, top with the toasted hazelnuts, and serve warm.

Herby Picnic Potato Salad

When I think of potato salad, I get an immediate visual of a schlopy white mayonnaise bomb in one of those vats at the grocery store deli; likely fifty-fifty mayo to potatoes and even less likely to be the safest thing to have sitting out at a picnic. However, there is something classically picnic-appropriate about a potato salad, or as a side dish at a backyard summer barbecue on a warm evening. Here, I toss the potatoes while still warm with their dressing, as the potatoes are most absorbent then. They roll around in a capery vinaigrette along with a little celery for crunch and some egg for classic's sake. I've been tempted to add shaved Parmesan here as well, but will leave that to your discretion. The salad is best at room temperature, so if you make it in advance, leave it out of the fridge for at least 30 minutes prior to serving.

---

2 pounds new potatoes (such as red, baby purple, baby golden, royals)

2 hard-boiled eggs

3 tablespoons capers

2 green onions, white and green parts, coarsely chopped

1 cup loosely packed basil leaves

⅓ cup flat-leaf parsley, plus more for garnish

¼ cup chopped chives, plus more for garnish

⅓ cup extra-virgin olive oil

2 tablespoons white wine vinegar

Sea salt and freshly ground pepper, to taste

3 celery stalks, finely diced

¼ teaspoon red pepper flakes

Put the potatoes in a large pot, cover them with water and bring the water up to a boil. Boil for 12 to 15 minutes until they are cooked through but not falling apart—just until you can easily pierce a sharp knife through the center. Drain.

Peel and chop the hard-boiled eggs.

In a food processor, blitz 2 tablespoons of the capers and their brine, green onions, basil, parsley, chives, oil, vinegar, and ½ teaspoon salt and ½ teaspoon pepper until you get a coarse vinaigrette. Quarter the potatoes and collect them in a large mixing bowl. Pour the vinaigrette over the just-cooled potatoes and gently toss to coat. It will look like a lot of dressing, but the potatoes soak it up as they sit. Chop up the remaining 1 tablespoon of the capers and stir them into the potatoes with the hard-boiled eggs, celery, and red pepper flakes. Taste for salt and pepper, garnish with additional parsley and chives, and serve at room temperature.

Kale Caesar *with* Cornbread Bits

Serves 4 to 6

Before the breadth and depth of my love for salads was as extensive as it is today, Caesar was what I knew. My dad and I had a favorite salad bar where the server would toss one to order, fresh and crisp, with the quintessential luscious dressing clinging to the fresh chopped romaine. And those buttery croutons! What is a Caesar without a crispy bit? While the classic can't be replaced, this is my version—no risky raw egg yolks and a crouton substitute of toasted cornbread bits for crunch and sweetness. A simple side salad for summer dinners outside that goes with just about anything. The sturdiness of kale begs for a dressing with a bit of constitution, which this one certainly has in its creaminess and kick from a touch of horseradish.

If you like to have extra dressing in the fridge, it can be easily increased by doubling everything besides the garlic clove and anchovy. I don't make a specific cornbread for this recipe, since it does not call for much. I grab a corn muffin when I am at a bakery or I buy a slice from my neighborhood deli. And, remember, it will crisp up better if it's a few days old.

DRESSING

1 large clove garlic, coarsely chopped

¼ cup extra-virgin olive oil

2 tablespoons good quality mayonnaise or veganaise

1 teaspoon prepared horseradish

2 teaspoon Worcestershire sauce

2 anchovies, or 1 teaspoon anchovy paste (optional)

¼ teaspoon sea salt

½ teaspoon freshly ground pepper

1 tablespoon chopped fresh parsley

¼ cup freshly squeezed lemon juice

—

1 cup (5 ounces) crumbled cornbread, preferably a few days old

2 teaspoons extra-virgin olive oil

1 small bunch kale, stemmed and chopped

3 cups chopped hearts of romaine

⅔ cup shaved Parmesan cheese

For the dressing, in a food processor or blender, add the garlic, olive oil, mayonnaise, horseradish, Worcestershire, anchovies, salt, pepper, parsley, and lemon juice. Give it a whirl until smooth. Keep in the fridge until ready to use.

Preheat the oven or toaster oven to 375°F. Spread the cornbread pieces on a parchment-lined baking sheet. Drizzle with the olive oil and toss gently with your hands to coat. Bake for 15 to 18 minutes until dry and crispy. Set aside to cool.

In a large salad bowl, combine the kale, romaine, and half the Parmesan. Toss with the desired amount of dressing. Sprinkle with the cornbread crispies and remaining Parmesan and serve.

The Last Meal Salad

Serves 4 to 6

I know, so morbid. The question of what would be included in your last meal often comes up when the topic of conversation turns to food. I sheepishly wait to go last, as the eye rolls are dramatic when you start describing your ideal salad. Yes, there would be fresh grainy bread with a crispy crust and top-of-the-line butter, a glass of a red wine I couldn't otherwise afford be it not my last, and a warm chocolate pudding cake with real peppermint ice cream; but yes, a giant salad would be present. Can't imagine going out any other way. Not because I'm trying to be goodie-two-shoes healthy girl, but honestly, big salads are my favorite meal. Not just greens and chopped raw vegetables, I am talking a variety of flavors and textures and creaminess and a delicious homemade dressing.

A last meal is composed of all your favorite things, right? This is a hodgepodge of some of my favorite things. The quality of the ingredients matters most. The avocado needs to be ripe, but not mushy, the leeks sautéed crispy but not oily, and the lettuce fresh and dried well so the dressing lightly coats each leaf. If it's going to be my last, it's going to be good.

2 teaspoons extra-virgin olive oil or coconut oil	1 cup pitted and halved cherries (or ⅓ cup dried, if out of season)
1 large leek, halved and cleaned	½ cup cooked black lentils
Sea salt	2 avocados, pitted and diced
4 cups (5 ounces) arugula	½ cup Marcona almonds, coarsely chopped
1 head (about 5 ounces) chopped red leaf lettuce	½ cup crumbled sheep milk feta
1 English cucumber, finely diced	Everyday Green Dressing (page 196)

In a large pan, heat the oil over medium heat. Slice the leek into thin half circles and add them to the hot pan. Add a pinch of salt and cook, stirring infrequently so the edges get crispy, 6 to 8 minutes. Remove from the heat and set aside to cool completely.

Wash and dry your greens well. Put them in a large salad bowl. Add the cucumber, cherries, lentils, half of the avocado, the almonds, and feta. Once cool, add all of the leeks. Toss everything with the dressing to taste. Top the salad with the remaining avocado, and serve immediately.

Lentil Tapenade

This is the tapenade or dip that you want to have in the fridge when people stop by. It holds up well and the olives add a ton of flavor to a bowl of lentils. It serves as a dip for crackers, as a sandwich or wrap filling, hot or cold, with some soft goat cheese, or to jazz up a weeknight salad. I'll throw a few spoonfuls into a green salad with a few sliced tomatoes and feta cheese. And, it's easy to make. If you can't find white balsamic, regular balsamic has the same flavor, it just makes everything a little more brown.

½ cup pitted and chopped Kalamata olives

2 tablespoons chopped fresh flat-leaf parsley

3 tablespoons chopped fresh basil

1 tablespoon chopped fresh oregano

2 Persian cucumbers, finely diced

⅓ cup minced red onion

2 tablespoons extra-virgin olive oil

1 cup cooked black or French green lentils

¼ to ½ teaspoon sea salt

½ teaspoon freshly ground pepper

1 tablespoon white balsamic vinegar

In a large mixing bowl, combine the olives, herbs, cucumbers, onion, and olive oil. Add the lentils, salt to taste, the pepper and stir to coat. Stir in the balsamic vinegar and adjust seasonings to taste.

Will keep, covered, in the fridge for 1 week.

Marrakesh Carrots

Avoid the dry, preshredded carrots at the market for this recipe, as the feathery crunch of freshly grated carrots really complements the other textures in this salad. And it's the perfect chance to use the grater blade on your food processor.

Having salads that I can store in the fridge for a couple of days is my best laid-plan for a quick meal. The easiest choice is not usually the healthiest, but keeping big batches of hearty salads like this on hand makes it easier. This salad packs well for long plane trips or an afternoon picnic. A hint on the dates: If you are lucky enough to find really moist ones, they are easier to chop cold; stick them in the fridge or freezer for 15 minutes before chopping. I list olive oil for sake of accessibility, but if you can get your hands on pistachio oil, that is excellent in its place.

When serving this salad for a dinner party, I'll sprinkle good-quality feta cheese on top to add a salty kick or some pomegranate seeds for color, if the season is right.

---

4 cups grated carrots

1½ cups garbanzo beans, rinsed and drained

7 Medjool dates, pitted and chopped

¼ cup minced red onion

4 green onions, white and light green parts, finely chopped

½ cup coarsely chopped cilantro

2½ tablespoons extra-virgin olive oil

Zest and juice of 2 limes

½ teaspoon ground cumin

¼ teaspoon freshly grated nutmeg

¼ teaspoon turmeric

Pinch of red pepper flakes

½ teaspoon sea salt

½ teaspoon freshly ground pepper

½ cup toasted pistachios

Crumbled feta cheese, for garnish (optional)

Pomegranate seeds, for garnish (optional)

In a large bowl, combine the carrots, garbanzo beans, dates, red onion, green onions, and cilantro.

In another bowl, whisk together the olive oil, zest and juice of the limes, cumin, nutmeg, turmeric, red pepper flakes, salt, and pepper.

Pour the dressing over the carrot salad and toss to coat. Sprinkle on the pistachios, feta cheese, and pomegranate seeds. Serve as is, or cover and chill in the fridge.

Mixed Greens *with* Beet *and* Walnut Puree

A beet, walnut, and goat cheese salad, in a different context. I did not invent this combination but will agree it goes together classically. The ingredients pair well together and in some form, they show up on a hearty handful of restaurant menus. Here, I am working off my multiyear obsession with hummus on everything to reinvent this salad. I make a puree a few of the salad ingredients, a mixture of the earthy beets and toasty walnuts brightened with a touch of vinegar and mustard. The pile of greens rests on top of that creamy puree so as you stab each bite, you get a little scoop of the puree on your fork. The texture may not be for everyone, but I like the contrast and it plates uniquely. This salad should be plated, not served family style, as it would be a giant mess with the puree tossed in. Save this one for a time when you and your guests have individual salad bowls.

DRESSING

1 teaspoon poppy seeds

¼ cup extra-virgin olive oil, divided

½ a small yellow onion, coarsely chopped

1 tablespoon honey

2 tablespoon white wine vinegar

2 teaspoons water

¼ teaspoon sea salt

½ teaspoon freshly ground pepper

—

3 large, whole roasted beets (see Note on page 65)

½ cup walnut pieces, toasted, plus more for garnish

1 tablespoon extra-virgin olive oil

1 tablespoon white wine vinegar

1 teaspoon Dijon mustard

5 ounces soft goat cheese (chèvre)

Sea salt and freshly ground papper

5 cups mixed greens

2 clementines, peeled and segmented

2 shallots, minced

Sea salt and pepper

For the dressing, warm a small saucepan over medium heat. Add the poppy seeds and toast in the dry pan for 3 minutes. Transfer them to a blender or food processor. Warm 2 teaspoons of the olive oil in the same pan, add the onion and sauté until translucent, about 3 minutes. To the blender, add the cooked onion, honey, vinegar, water, salt, and pepper and process until mostly smooth. With the motor running, drizzle in the remaining olive oil. Set aside until ready to use.

Continued

Coarsely chop two of the beets. Slice the other one into small wedges and reserve for the garnish. In a clean processor or high-powered blender, puree the chopped beets with the walnuts, olive oil, vinegar, mustard, 2 ounces of the chevre, and a few pinches of sea salt and pepper. You want it thick and mostly smooth with a bit of texture. This step can be done up to 2 days in advance.

Toss the greens with the clementines, shallot, and the desired amount of dressing; then, crumble on the remaining 3 ounces of chevre. Prepare each bowl with a pillow of the beet walnut puree and top with the dressed greens (offset so you can see the puree beneath). Sprinkle on a few walnuts and the reserved beets for garnish.

Note: To roast beets, preheat the oven to 425°F. Remove the beet greens, rub the outsides with a thin coat of olive oil and wrap all of them in a foil package. Bake them on the middle rack for 45 minutes or until you can pierce to the center with a knife. Remove to cool completely and the skins will peel right off easily with your hands or a paring knife.

Grilled Zucchini Salad *with* Cilantro Pepita Pesto

When we go to the beach, I get a bit carried away with the snacks. An ample lunch and snacks allow us to stay until our shoulders are sun-kissed. I brought this salad to our last Fourth of July beach day—a day we plan to park it in the sand from noon until the sun goes down. I packed up my largest Tupperware of this salad, crumbled my favorite feta cheese on top for a salty punch, and stuck a few spoons in the side of the cooler. I won't forget the visual of my best friends and me all gathered at the beach in the late afternoon, passing around the dish and filling our bellies with a nice change from the sandwich and chips that typically sustain us on a long beach day. It's a salad worth sharing.

The zucchini can be grilled in advance, so if you have the grill on and you're thinking ahead, throw on the zucchini and you'll have them on hand when you want to make the salad. An indoor grill pan works, too. I use sweet paprika here, but if you have smoked on hand, I like that, too. The pesto should make a bit more than you'll need to dress the quinoa, but it makes a great salad dressing thinned out with a bit more citrus.

½ cup quinoa

1 cup low-sodium vegetable broth

5 to 6 zucchini (about 1½ pounds)

1½ tablespoon extra-virgin olive oil

1 teaspoon sweet paprika

½ teaspoon sea salt

—

PESTO

2 cloves garlic

2 green onions, white and light green parts

½ cup toasted pepitas, plus more for garnish

½ teaspoon sea salt

1 jalapeño, mostly seeded

1 bunch of cilantro

Zest and juice of 2 large limes, about ¼ cup fresh juice

⅓ cup extra-virgin olive oil

½ cup coarsely chopped cilantro

½ cup crumbled sheep's milk feta, plus more for garnish

Rinse the quinoa in a fine mesh strainer. In a medium saucepan, combine the quinoa and broth. Bring the broth to a boil, down to a gentle simmer, cover, and cook for 15 minutes. Fluff the quinoa, turn off the heat, and leave the lid ajar. Set aside to cool completely.

Preheat your grill or grill pan to medium heat. Quarter the zucchini lengthwise into spears (if on the larger side, cut lengthwise into sixths). Drizzle them with the olive oil, and sprinkle with sweet paprika and salt; toss to coat with your hands, being sure all sides are covered. Grill the spears for 7 to 10 minutes, flipping them halfway through, or until al dente. Remove to cool completely and cut into 1-inch chunks.

To make the pesto, pulse the garlic, green onions, pepitas, and sea salt in a food processor. Add the jalapeño, cilantro, and lime juice and run the processor to combine. With the motor running, drizzle in the olive oil and a splash of water. Taste and adjust as you wish: add more citrus juice and/or salt to brighten it, and water if you prefer it thinner. The pesto can be made up to 3 days in advance and kept covered in the fridge.

In a large bowl, combine the quinoa and a few heaping spoonfuls of the pesto, stirring to combine. Add the chopped cilantro, zucchini, and feta and gently mix. Add more pesto to taste and garnish with a bit more feta. Serve at room temperature or keep covered and chilled until ready to eat.

Roasted Asparagus Bowl

For years, I've been eating asparagus exclusively in spears, thin or thick stalks, either grilled or roasted whole. They plate well and come out tender, but chopping them into smaller pieces for roasting gives more caramelized edges, and who doesn't like more caramelized edges? The skinny sort won't do here; you need a medium-size asparagus stalk that can hold its shape under the heat and still toss well in a bowl with a speckle of lentils and a vinaigrette.

French green lentils look like the caviar of lentils and hold their shape. Add shavings of your favorite cheese if you wish—a nutty Gruyère or salty pecorino would be lovely.

½ cup black or French green lentils

1½ cups low sodium vegetable broth

2 bunches (about 1½ pounds) asparagus, medium thickness

1½ to 2 tablespoons extra-virgin olive oil

½ teaspoon sea salt

½ teaspoon dried Italian herb blend or oregano

—

DRESSING

1 teaspoon Dijon mustard

1 shallot, minced (about 2 tablespoons)

2 tablespoons extra-virgin olive oil

1½ tablespoons white balsamic vinegar

Sea salt and freshly ground pepper

½ cup toasted walnut pieces

½ cup chopped fresh herbs (basil, chives, parsley, or a combination)

Place rack in the middle of the oven and preheat to 450°F.

Rinse the lentils and add them with the broth to a pot. Bring them to a boil, back to a simmer, and cook for 20 minutes or until just tender. Drain any excess liquid.

Snap off the dry ends of the asparagus. Cut them at a diagonal into 2-inch pieces. Spread them on a large rimmed baking sheet in a single layer, using two sheets if needed to avoid crowding the pan. Drizzle over 1½ tablespoons of the olive oil, add the salt and the dried herbs and toss to coat, adding more oil as needed to make sure everything is thinly coated. Roast for 13 to 15 minutes until the edges brown.

For the dressing, in a small bowl, whisk together the Dijon mustard, minced shallot, olive oil, vinegar, and a pinch of salt and pepper. In your serving bowl, toss the lentils, asparagus, walnuts, and herbs with the vinaigrette. Serve warm or chilled.

Spanish Chopped Salad *with* Walnut Paprika Vinaigrette

Serves 4

I lived in Spain for about six months during college. One of my best friends and I lived with a family in a small city an hour outside of Madrid. We went to school to sharpen our Spanish and traveled by train on the weekends enjoying tapas and the infamous late-night life. On a budget, we made meals of those Spanish tapas enjoyed bar side, and while there is nothing traditionally Spanish about this salad, the zesty paprika-spiked vinaigrette here reminds me of those flavors. This side salad goes well with grilled meats or white fish, but could easily pass for a light lunch on its own. The simple key to a good chopped salad is to get all the pieces chopped super small—almost like you could eat the salad with a spoon. This recipe yields just enough vinaigrette for this salad. Double it if you would like extra on hand.

VINAIGRETTE

1 clove garlic

3 tablespoons red wine vinegar or sherry vinegar

3 tablespoons toasted walnut pieces

½ teaspoon smoked paprika

2 teaspoons honey

2 tablespoons chopped parsley

⅓ cup extra-virgin olive oil

½ teaspoon sea salt

Freshly ground pepper

—

1 head romaine, cleaned, dried, and chopped

2 cups baby spinach

¼ of a red onion, thinly sliced

⅓ toasted walnut pieces

1 cup halved cherry tomatoes

1 small, finely diced apple

1 cup finely diced cucumber

2 hard-boiled eggs, chopped

½ cup cooked lentils

1 cup (4 ounces) shaved Manchego cheese

For the vinaigrette, in a blender or food processor, combine the garlic, red wine vinegar, walnuts, smoked paprika, honey, parsley, olive oil, salt, and pepper. Blend for 30 seconds or until smooth. Taste for seasoning. Set aside in the fridge until ready to use. The dressing can be made up to 3 days in advance.

Put the romaine and spinach in a large salad bowl. Add the onion, walnuts, tomatoes, apple, cucumber, hard-boiled eggs, and lentils to the bowl. Dress the salad with the desired amount of the vinaigrette and toss to coat. Add the Manchego, give the salad another toss, and serve.

Spiced Sweet Potato Chips *and* Crème Fraîche Dip

Serves 4

No matter the finesse of your knife skills, these are not worth making without a mandoline. You need very thin, even slices for these homemade chips to bake evenly. Too thick and they'll never crisp up. I have made these on a nonstick baking sheet and a plain stainless steel with different results. If using a nonstick pan, the timing is a little more sensitive, meaning the darker surface makes them cook quicker and they'll turn from toasted to burned in a moment. But in either case, these don't take long at all, so keep your eye on them.

While not the biggest blue cheese fan, I do find it makes a lovely pair with sweet potatoes. The dip can be made in advance and kept covered in the fridge for up to a week.

---

1 large sweet potato (about ¾ pound)

1½ tablespoons olive oil or melted coconut oil

½ to 1 teaspoon sea salt

¼ teaspoon cinnamon

¼ teaspoon cayenne

¼ teaspoon chili powder

¼ teaspoon smoked paprika

—

DIP

⅓ cup crème fraîche

1 teaspoon freshly squeezed lemon juice

2 teaspoons fresh thyme leaves

¼ cup (2 ounces) crumbled blue cheese or gorgonzola

Pinch of freshly ground pepper

Preheat the oven to 400°F. Line two rimmed baking sheets with parchment paper.

Slice the potato using a mandoline, into ¹⁄₁₆-inch slices. In a large mixing bowl, combine the oil, salt, cinnamon, cayenne, chili powder, and smoked paprika. Add the sliced potatoes and toss to coat, being sure every slice has some oil on it. Divide the potatoes between the two sheets and arrange them in a single layer with the least amount of overlap possible. Put the sheets in the oven, turn down the heat to 375°F, and bake for 10 minutes. Remove the sheets and flip the potatoes, rotate the sheet to alternative racks, and bake another 6 to 9 minutes until the edges are just browned. Allow them to cool to completely crisp up.

For the dip, put the crème fraîche in a bowl with the lemon juice, thyme leaves, blue cheese, and pepper. Mash everything together with the back of a fork. Chips are best enjoyed within a day.

Summer Tomato Salad

Serves 4

We have a local farm that sells all sorts of organic produce and manages our CSA program. Some of the items come in from other farms, but a few of the items grown on their premises are without a doubt the best around. People line up for the strawberries—picked every day and sold out by noon. Their tomatoes come in all shapes, sizes, and colors, but I just love the ruby red beefsteak ones. This is hardly a recipe, as wonderful tomatoes need little fuss, especially in the summer when a bowl of fresh dressed tomatoes makes a gorgeous side.

I may say this a lot, but please save this salad for when you have farm-fresh, summery-sweet and juicy tomatoes. It's essentially all the salad stands on. Simple recipes are only amazing if you start with the best-quality produce. This side salad does beautifully with some fresh, raw corn kernels, a poached egg on top, and warm crusty bread to make it more of a meal.

1 small red onion

⅓ cup white wine vinegar

1 tablespoon natural cane sugar

½ teaspoon sea salt

2 pounds ripe tomatoes, assorted colors and sizes

2 large avocados

—

DRESSING

2 teaspoons Dijon mustard

2 tablespoons white balsamic vinegar

¼-½ teaspoon of sea salt

½ teaspoon freshly ground pepper

¼ cup extra-virgin olive oil

—

Flaked sea salt, such as Maldon

1 cup microgreens

Shave the onion very thin and put the slices in a mixing bowl. In a saucepan, warm the vinegar, sugar, and salt to medium heat. Pour the warm vinegar mixture over the onions, toss them to coat, and put them in the fridge for at least 30 minutes and up to overnight.

Slice your tomatoes alternately in wedges and slices, offering a variety of shapes and sizes. Peel and cut the avocado into quarters, or sixths if on the larger side.

For the dressing, whisk together the mustard, vinegar, salt, pepper, and olive oil.

Drain the onions. In a mixing bowl, toss the tomato, avocado, and desired amount of the pickled onion with the dressing. Top with a generous sprinkling of flaky salt and the microgreens.

the sprouted kitchen bowl + spoon

The Greeny Bowl

I have an affinity for monochromatic colors, be it in home decor, an outfit, or food. This salad was a fridge cleanout turned repeat favorite and I keep everything a shade of green. A big bowl of different shades of green presents beautifully.

Roasted brussels sprouts are a treat warm from the oven, but cooled down, they add some nice texture and bulk to this salad. You could add another heart of romaine if you need to stretch the salad for more people.

¾ pound brussels sprouts

1½ tablespoons extra-virgin olive oil

1 tablespoon maple syrup

½ teaspoon paprika

Sea salt and freshly ground pepper

2 hearts of romaine, chopped

3 cups mixed greens

1 pear (Bartlett, Comice, or Anjou), diced

1 avocado, diced

3 green onions, white and green parts, thinly sliced

⅓ cup toasted pepitas

½ cup shaved Parmesan

—

DRESSING

1 clove garlic, minced

2 teaspoons maple syrup

2 teaspoon Dijon mustard

1 teaspoon dried Italian herbs

3 tablespoons white wine vinegar

⅓ cup extra-virgin olive oil

Sea salt and freshly ground pepper

Preheat the oven to 400°F and line a baking sheet with parchment or foil for easy clean up (maple syrup gets sticky). Halve or quarter the brussels sprouts, depending on size. Place them in a bowl, and toss them with the olive oil, maple syrup, paprika, and a few pinches of salt. Spread them in a single layer on the baking sheet and roast for 25 minutes, until the edges are browned. Remove and set aside to cool completely. This can be done 1 day in advance.

Add the romaine and the mixed greens to a large salad bowl. Add the pear, avocado, green onions, half of the pepitas, and ¼ cup of the Parmesan, and the brussels sprouts to the bowl.

For the dressing, in a small blender or by hand, whisk together the garlic, maple syrup, mustard, herbs, vinegar, olive oil, and a pinch of salt and pepper until combined. Dress the salad and toss to mix well. Garnish with the remaining pepitas and Parmesan and serve.

Za'atar Roasted Carrots

These generously seasoned, sweet roasted carrots remind me that this vegetable can take on such a variety of spices. The Middle Eastern spice za'atar is typically a blend of thyme, sumac, and sesame seeds. While maybe not a spice blend you stock in your cupboard, it's wonderful mixed into labneh or Greek yogurt for a dip, with greens, feta, and chickpeas for a side salad, or as a marinade for grilled kebabs. Or maybe you'll be reserving it for a few batches of these savory roasted carrots. These make a great side for the Herbed Falafel Bowl (page 115), or they can be chopped into smaller pieces and tossed with some cooked quinoa for something a little more hearty.

I try to pick bundles of carrots on the smaller side so I only have to slice them lengthwise before roasting. Larger carrots work fine, just slice them crosswise as well to get manageable pieces on your roasting sheet.

1½ pounds young carrots, cleaned	Sea salt and freshly ground pepper
1 tablespoon extra-virgin olive oil	2 to 3 tablespoons tahini
2 tablespoons freshly squeezed orange juice	Juice of ½ lemon
2 teaspoons fresh orange zest	⅓ cup crumbled feta
2 teaspoons za'atar	1 tablespoon toasted sesame seeds
	¼ cup chopped flat-leaf parsley

Place a rack in the upper third of the oven and preheat to 400°F.

Trim the carrots. Cut them in half lengthwise and, if they're on the larger side, crosswise on a diagonal as well. Mix together the olive oil, orange juice, zest, za'atar, and a few pinches of sea salt. Toss the carrots in the spice mixture and spread them on a rimmed baking sheet. Bake for 22 to 25 minutes until the edges begin to brown. Mix together the tahini and lemon juice. Drizzle the carrots with the tahini mixture and sprinkle with the feta, sesame seeds, parsley, and a pinch of freshly ground pepper.

BIG BOWLS

A bowl, at least in the context of this book, is less about
necessity or appropriateness than it is about comfort
and ease. Comfort is like a warm bowl of noodles with
just enough creaminess to satisfy, or the familiarity of
combining your favorite grains and vegetables in a bowl
with a new delicious sauce—a thai-spiced broth that you
can lap up with a spoon or a big pot of tortilla soup with a
table full of toppings for an impromptu dinner with your
favorite people. I chose bowls as a theme for this book
because I believe they elicit something from us as we think
about our place in the kitchen or at a table. Cooking, dining,
entertaining—it's all a lot less serious and much more
communal and personal than we sometimes allow it to be.
A bowl reminds me of that. It's a time to catch up and to eat
something nourishing to pull us through full days.

Ahi Poke Bowls

Serves 4

I only started making these bowls once I found a place to get moderately priced, gorgeous ruby-colored, extremely fresh ahi. I pick it up the day it is cut and packed and eat it that very night to make sure it's as good as it gets. You want to make sure your fish is labeled "sushi grade" to ensure it's optimal to eat raw. Making sushi at home is a bit of a process, but putting this fresh sashimi and rice in a bowl makes it quick and less expensive.

You can replace the vinegar with lime juice in this recipe, but be sure not to marinate the fish for too long or these acidic ingredients will begin to "cook" the fish. The prep is so easy, it shouldn't take you long either way.

I serve this with the Snap Pea and Edamame Salad (page 42), and adding it to the same bowl adds a great crunchy texture.

1½ cups short-grain brown or white rice

1½ pounds sushi-grade ahi tuna

3 tablespoons low-sodium soy sauce

2 teaspoon toasted sesame oil

1 tablespoon rice wine vinegar

Wasabi paste, Sriracha sauce, or chile pepper flakes

2 green onions, white and green parts, thinly sliced

2 large, ripe avocados

Freshly ground pepper

1½ tablespoons sesame seeds

4 to 6 sheets dried nori, for garnish

Rinse the rice in a fine-mesh strainer. Cook the rice according to instructions or in a rice cooker.

With a sharp knife, cut the ahi into 1-inch cubes. In a large bowl, whisk together the soy sauce, sesame oil, vinegar, and a bit of wasabi, Sriracha, or chile flakes to taste. Add the ahi and green onions and stir gently to combine. This much can be done up to 1 hour in advance. Keep chilled.

Just before serving, pit and dice the avocado into small cubes. Gently stir them into the ahi with a generous pinch of pepper and sesame seeds.

Arrange your poke bowl with a generous scoop of rice, ahi mixture, and crumbled, dried nori on top. Serve with more soy and wasabi on the side.

Slivered Veggie *and* Soba Salad *with* Mapled Tofu

Serves 4

I usually resist filling my kitchen drawers with gadgets I won't use; but there were too many instances when I wanted a julienne peeler and now I regret waiting so long to purchase one. This dish is mostly vegetables with a bit of noodles, and that is all thanks to the "vegetable noodles" made with the julienne peeler. You could make this dish with grated vegetables or thin slices on a mandoline, but the peeler gets them a similar size to the soba, so the textures marry perfectly. If you like a more noodled salad, just double the amount of soba.

Take the liberty to swap in a different protein—some tempeh or chicken sautéed in the same ingredients would be a nice alternative. The dressing here is similar to the Tahini Citrus Miso Dressing on page 203, just a bit lighter without the tahini. Either one works great for a crisp, fresh salad, perfect for picnics or work/school lunches.

---

14 ounces extra-firm tofu

2 tablespoons coconut oil

2 teaspoon low-sodium soy sauce

1 tablespoon maple syrup

Freshly ground pepper

3 ounces soba noodles

1 red bell pepper

3 carrots, peeled

1 English cucumber

1 bunch of cilantro, coarsely chopped

2 green onions, thinly sliced

2 tablespoons toasted sesame seeds, for garnish

1 large avocado

—

DRESSING

1 tablespoon yellow miso paste

1 (3-inch) piece of fresh ginger, peeled and grated

1 teaspoon honey

Zest and juice of 2 limes

1 tablespoon toasted sesame oil

1 teaspoon Sriracha sauce

Drain the tofu and press out the excess liquid between layers of a folded clean dishcloth. In a large skillet, heat the coconut oil over medium heat. Chop the tofu into ½-inch cubes and add them to the hot pan. Sauté gently until the edges begin to brown. Add the soy sauce, maple syrup, and pepper. Stir and cook for 6 to 8 minutes longer, until the edges are crisp. Set aside to cool.

Cook the soba noodles until al dente, rinse with cold water, and drain. Seed and slice the bell pepper into thin strips. Use a julienne peeler to make long strips from the carrot and cucumber, keeping away from the inner seedy part of the cucumber. Put the noodles and prepared vegetables into a large mixing bowl.

For the dressing, whisk together the miso, ginger, honey, lime zest and juice, sesame oil, and Sriracha. This much can be done up to 2 days in advance and kept covered in the fridge.

When ready to serve, pour the dressing over the veggies and noodles, add the chopped cilantro and toss to coat. Top the bowl with the green onions, sesame seeds, and tofu. Serve each portion with a quarter of an avocado.

BUILDING A BOWL

"Bowl foods" do not always need recipes—they are often a combination of your favorite things, what may be in the fridge, or a chance to use what is in season. I like to mix colors and textures, sweetness and spice, cooked and raw ingredients, and always a sauce. Think mostly plants, a whole grain, lean protein, a healthy fat for garnish and a simple sauce of your choice. I've included a few ideas to get you started on composing bowls of your own.

GRAINS:
rice, quinoa, millet, noodles, bulgar, spelt . . .

WELL-SEASONED PROTEIN:
eggs, tofu, tempeh, chicken, fish . . .

LEGUMES:
beans or lentils . . .

GREENS:
spinach, kale, lettuces, collards,
Swiss chard, broccoli, cabbage . . .

VEGETABLES:
grilled, braised, shredded, cooked, and
raw for crunch . . .

TOPPINGS:
cheese, toasted or candied nuts,
crispy bread crumbs, avacado . . .

SAUCE!

Seared Albacore Niçoise

Serves 4

I started making this meal for friends because it has a family-style component to it that I really like. I arrange all the parts of a traditional Niçoise salad in a wide, shallow bowl, letting everyone serve themselves, and taking as much or as little of each element as they choose. I find albacore to be an affordable and inoffensive seafood choice for most, and it can be forgiving to cook, as it only needs a very quick sear to cook properly. If you are not one for albacore, you can substitute grilled chicken or tofu in its place, maybe even offer both—any of which make a light meal option.

1½ pounds sushi-grade albacore tuna

3 tablespoons grapeseed or other high-heat cooking oil

1½ teaspoons herbs de Provence

1 teaspoon dried oregano

Sea salt and freshly ground pepper

1 pound haricots verts

1½ tablespoons extra-virgin olive oil

Zest and juice of 1 small Meyer lemon

2 tablespoons chopped dill

1½ cups, or 1 (14-ounce) can, cooked cannelini beans, rinsed and drained

½ cup shaved Parmesan

1 pound boiled or steamed baby new potatoes

1 pound tomatoes, cut in wedges

3 hard-boiled eggs, peeled and quartered

½ cup assorted pitted olives, coarsely chopped

⅓ cup fresh chopped flat-leaf parsley

—

VINAIGRETTE

1 tablespoon Dijon mustard

1 teaspoon honey

2 tablespoons minced shallot

1 sprig of fresh thyme

½ teaspoon sea salt

½ teaspoon freshly ground pepper

3 tablespoons white wine or sherry vinegar

½ cup extra-virgin olive oil

Dab the tuna steaks dry with a cloth or paper towel, rub them with a thin coat of the grapeseed oil (about 1 tablespoon), and sprinkle with the herbs de Provence, oregano, and liberally with sea salt and pepper. Allow them to sit at room temperature for 20 to 30 minutes while you prepare the other ingredients.

For the vinaigrette, whisk together the mustard, honey, shallot, thyme, salt, pepper, and vinegar. Whisk in the extra-virgin olive oil. This can be made up to 3 days in advance.

Bring a pot of water to a boil and prepare an ice bath. Blanch the haricots verts for 1 to 2 minutes until vibrant green. Immediately dunk in the ice bath, then drain. In a mixing bowl, whisk together the olive oil, lemon zest and juice, and the dill;

season with salt and pepper. Add the haricots verts, cannelini beans, and Parmesan and toss to coat. Set aside in the fridge until ready to use.

Cut the potatoes into halves or quarters, depending on size.

Heat the remaining 2 tablespoons of the grapeseed oil in a large, heavy skillet over medium-high heat. Once hot, add the seasoned albacore and cook for 2 minutes on each side for medium rare, depending on thickness. Press on the center; it should have some give to it. You don't want the fish cooked through. Remove and set it aside to rest for a few minutes. Thinly slice the fish.

Assemble each ingridient separately on a large family style platter, so everyone may compose their own bowls. Drizzle the potatoes, tomatoes, and fish with the vinaigrette and garnish with chopped parsley. Serve with wedges of crusty garlic bread and enjoy.

Barbecue Tempeh, Greens, *and* Cauliflower "Couscous"

Serves 4 to 6

Although this recipe uses three different pans, I think it's worth it; and if you remember to marinate the tempeh ahead, it's a great weeknight meal. Cauliflower "couscous" or "rice" is a great use of this often overlooked vegetable and a wonderful replacement for grains. A few pulses in the processor and a chunky head of cauliflower takes on the texture of couscous (or rice) and the flavor of anything you choose to add. If you don't have a food processor, an intentional chop with the knife will do.

Tempeh is a fermented soy product, said to have more nutritional value than tofu and a much meatier texture. For the omnivores, chicken works as a replacement; I also like this marinade with salmon on the grill.

½ cup barbecue sauce

½ cup orange juice

2½ tablespoons low-sodium soy sauce

2 tablespoons apple cider vinegar

16 ounces tempeh

—

1 small head (about 1 pound) cauliflower

2 tablespoons ghee or unsalted butter

½ yellow onion, finely diced

1 to 2 teaspoons garlic powder

¼ teaspoon freshly grated nutmeg

Sea salt, to taste

2 tablespoons coconut oil

2 tablespoons extra-virgin olive oil

3 cloves garlic, minced

6 cups stemmed and chopped Swiss chard

1 tablespoon freshly squeezed lemon juice

Sea salt and freshly ground pepper

½ cup chopped flat-leaf parsley

½ cup grated Parmesan cheese, plus more for serving

Roasted and salted peanuts, coarsely chopped (optional)

Mix together the barbecue sauce, orange juice, soy sauce, and vinegar in a shallow tray (an 8-inch square pan works great). Slice the tempeh in half horizontally, and then into triangles (about sixteen ¼-inch triangles) and lay them in the marinade, spooning some over the top. Let them sit for at least 1 hour, preferably overnight, flipping occasionally.

Cut the cauliflower into florets. In a food processor, pulse the florets just a few times to get the texture of a rough couscous. Heat the ghee over medium heat in a large skillet, add the onion, and cook until translucent, about 4 minutes. Add the cauliflower, garlic powder, nutmeg, and sea salt and sauté for 5 to 7 minutes to warm through. Cover and set aside.

Heat your grill, grill pan, or cast-iron pan to medium-high heat. Brush the grates or pan with coconut oil. Grill the tempeh for 5 minutes on each side, brushing with the marinade throughout cooking, reserving some for serving.

Meanwhile, make the greens. Warm the olive oil in a large skillet, add the garlic, and sauté until fragrant, about 1 minute. Add the Swiss chard and sauté for 2 to 3 minutes to wilt and warm through. Stir in the lemon juice and a pinch of salt and pepper.

Stir the parsley and Parmesan into the cauliflower and taste for salt and pepper. Brush the tempeh with the remaining marinade. Serve each bowl with a mound of the cauliflower couscous, grilled tempeh, and a side of greens. Serve with a sprinkle of Parmesan, the peanuts, and extra barbeque sauce on the side.

Caribbean Bowl *with* Jerk-Seasoned White Fish *and* Tropical Fruit Salsa

Serves 4

A new set of spices is a welcomed change to my quotidian seafood routine of lemon and herbs around here. This is another great meal where everyone can build their bowl with as much bright fruit salsa as they wish. The spice blend is a quick and easy one with a more understated jerk-type flavor. If you don't stock these spices, most markets sell a number of brands of jerk seasoning blends already made up. I don't find the choice of white fish pivotal here—maybe you prefer a meatier mahi-mahi or something light like cod. The timing will vary on type and thickness that you purchase. Look into the sustainable choices in your area. I've even used wild salmon when it's in season, and, while not Caribbean in the least, it works.

½ pound dried black beans, soaked overnight

1 jalapeño, mostly seeded

2 bay leaves

1 cup vegetable broth

Sea salt

1 cup brown rice

—

SALSA

1 shallot, minced (about 2 tablespoons)

3 tablespoons freshly squeezed lime juice

2 ripe mangos

2 large avocados

1 cup peeled, diced papaya

½ cup chopped cilantro

Freshly ground pepper

—

JERK SEASONING

1 teaspoon cumin

1 teaspoon chili powder

½ teaspoon garlic powder

½ teaspoon allspice

½ teaspoon curry powder

¼ teaspoon cinnamon

Pinch of red pepper flakes

Sea salt and freshly ground pepper

2 tablespoons orange juice

1½ pounds white fish (cod, mahi-mahi, sole)

—

2 tablespoons coconut oil

1 ripe plantain

Chopped green onions, white and light green parts, for garnish

Drain the soaking beans. Put them in a pot with the jalapeño and bay leaves and fill the pot with water to cover the beans by 2 inches. Bring the water to a simmer and cook the beans, uncovered, for 50 to 60 minutes, until tender. When the water has mostly cooked off, add the broth. When the beans are cooked, discard the jalapeño and bay leaves, add a few pinches of salt, cover, and set aside. The pot should not be dry; you want a bit of broth in the pot. The beans can be made up to 2 days in advance.

Cook the rice according to package instructions.

Meanwhile, prepare the salsa. Put the shallot and lime juice in a mixing bowl. Peel and pit the mangos and avocados and cut into small cubes. Add them and the papaya to the mixing bowl along with the chopped cilantro and a pinch of salt and pepper. Stir to mix. Cover and set aside in the fridge.

Preheat the oven to 375°F. The fish can also be grilled.

For the jerk seasoning, mix the cumin, chili powder, garlic powder, allspice, curry powder, cinnamon, red pepper flakes, and a pinch of salt and pepper together in a small bowl. Add the orange juice to make a spice paste. Arrange the fish on a parchment-lined baking sheet, skin-side down (if the skin is on). Brush the paste well into the flesh. Bake the fish for 12 to 15 minutes, depending on the thickness, until just cooked through.

Heat the coconut oil in a small skillet over medium-high heat. Peel and slice the plantain into ½-inch-thick slices on a generous diagonal. Give the slices a gentle smash with the side of a knife, sprinkle them with salt and pepper, and fry for 3 minutes per side until golden.

Serve each bowl with beans, a little bean broth, a scoop of the rice, portion of the fish, fruit salsa, and a few plantains; sprinkle with green onions and serve.

Lentil *and* Rice Bowls *with* Summer Vegetable Kebabs

Serves 4

This recipe has a traditional start for the Lebanese staple called *mujaddara*, lentils and rice, that I've tweaked a little bit for this bowl. It's pretty simple and can even be made a few days in advance, as can the sauce, and then you may grill or broil your kebabs when you're ready. It's the perfect al fresco meal, easy for a group, and I'll often throw whatever vegetables are in the crisper that could handle a char on the grill because the sauce goes well on just about everything. The sauce, a spicy-sweet roasted red pepper and walnut spread called *muhammara*, is truly what makes this bowl special. This amount of *muhammara* will get you through this meal, but I usually double it to have on hand for wraps and veggie dip. The feta adds a nice salty topping, but you have an excellent dairy and gluten-free bowl without it, so leave it off if you wish.

SAUCE (MUHAMMARA)

2 cloves garlic

2 roasted red bell peppers, jarred or fresh

¾ cup toasted walnuts

3 Medjool dates, pitted

2 tablespoons red wine vinegar

1 teaspoon sea salt

1 teaspoon freshly ground pepper

1½ teaspoons smoked paprika

1 teaspoon ground cumin

3 tablespoons extra-virgin olive oil

—

LENTILS (MUJADDARA)

¾ cup French green lentils

1 teaspoon sea salt

5½ cups of water

1 cup brown basmati rice

3 cups coarsely chopped baby spinach

1 tablespoon butter or ghee

2 tablespoons olive oil

2 yellow onions, halved and thinly sliced

Sea salt and pepper

—

KEBABS

½ pound small potatoes, halved

3 tablespoons extra-virgin olive oil

2 teaspoons garlic powder

Pinch of cayenne

1 small eggplant, cut into 1-inch chunks

2 bell peppers, orange and yellow, cut into 1-inch squares

½ red onion, cut into 1-inch squares

Sea salt and pepper

½ cup crumbled feta cheese, for garnish

For the sauce, in a food processor, pulse the garlic to mince. Add the red peppers, walnuts, dates, vinegar, salt, pepper, smoked paprika, cumin, and olive oil; run the processor until smooth. The sauce can be kept, covered, in the fridge for up to 2 weeks.

Preheat the oven to 400°F.

Put lentils, ½ teaspoon of the salt, and 4 cups of the water in a large pot and bring to a boil. Reduce heat and simmer lentils just until cooked, about 20 minutes. Drain lentils and set aside.

Add rice, the remaining ½ teaspoon of the salt, and 1½ cups water to the pot. Put it over medium heat and bring to a boil. When the water boils, cover, transfer to the oven, and cook for 17 minutes. Remove from the oven, uncover, fluff with a fork, and stir in the spinach to wilt. Set aside.

While the rice is cooking, heat a large sauté pan over medium heat and add butter and 2 tablespoons olive oil. When the butter has melted, add the onions and sauté. Cook about 15 minutes until the onions are very soft and browned. Raise heat to high and cook 3 to 4 minutes longer, until the bottom layer of onions has charred; try not to overstir so they get crisp. Combine rice, lentils, baby spinach, and onions in a large serving bowl and keep covered until your kebabs are ready. This much can be done 2 to 3 days in advance and warmed when ready to serve.

Preheat your grill or broiler.

Put the potatoes in a pot. Cover them with water, bring to a boil, and cook just until fork tender, about 10 minutes. Drain and let cool.

In a large mixing bowl, combine the oil, garlic powder, cayenne, and a few pinches of salt and pepper. Add the potatoes, eggplant, bell pepper, and onion and toss to coat. Thread the vegetables, alternating colors onto 8 to 10 skewers; reserve any excess oil for basting.

Oil your grill or prepare a parchment-lined baking sheet if broiling. Cook, rotating occasionally, until the vegetables are tender, 8 to 10 minutes.

Serve your bowls with a big scoop of the lentils and rice, a few kebabs, *muhummara*, and a sprinkle of feta.

Creamy Mushroom Pasta *with* Frizzled Leeks

Serves 4

This is *Sprouted Kitchen* comfort food, and we'll sit in silence for the first few bites, tangling our fork in the noodles, enjoying the creaminess that warms the belly. A riff on a recipe from *Bon Appétit*, but here, the bacon is swapped out for mushrooms, adding a few more spices and a different noodle. It comes together relatively quickly but doesn't taste like it did. I call for 12 ounces of pasta because I am a promoter of smaller pasta portions served alongside a big green salad and a slice of toasted, crusty bread. You could add some chicken sausage or the full pound of pasta if you like a heartier bowlful. The sauce will stretch a bit.

20 ounces mushrooms (crimini, button, or a mix), cleaned and stemmed

1 teaspoon sea salt

2 leeks, white and light green parts

1 tablespoon unsalted butter or ghee

½ cup dry white wine (or vegetable stock)

¾ cup heavy cream

2 teaspoons fresh thyme leaves, plus more for garnish

½ teaspoon red pepper flakes

Freshly grated nutmeg

12 ounces spaghetti (brown rice and whole wheat noodles work as well)

½ cup freshly grated Parmesan cheese

Zest of 2 lemons

½ cup chopped flat-leaf parsley

Bring a large pot of salted water to a boil.

Chop the mushrooms into a small dice. Heat a large, heavy skillet over medium heat. Add the mushrooms and salt to the dry pan and cook, stirring occasionally, until most of the liquid has released from the mushrooms and they have reduced to half their volume, about 10 minutes. While the mushrooms cook down, prepare the leeks. Clean and slice the leeks into thin half moons. In another pan, warm the butter over medium heat. Add the leeks, pinch of salt, and cook, stirring infrequently to get brown bits, for about 8 to 10 minutes.

When the mushroom pan is nearly dry, add the wine and stir for another minute. Cook for two minutes to reduce. Add the cream, thyme, red pepper flakes, a grating of nutmeg, ¼ teaspoon salt and simmer for 5 minutes to cook down.

Cook your pasta until al dente. Drain and reserve 1 cup of the pasta water. To the sauce in the mushroom pan, add ¼ cup of the pasta water, half of the Parmesan, the lemon zest, and noodles and toss to coat. Turn off the heat and add pasta water as needed to distribute the sauce. The sauce will thicken as it cools.

Top each portion with a scoop of the leeks, more Parmesan, and generous handful of parsley, and serve immediately.

Curried Sweet Potato Soup *with* Crispy Black Lentils

Serves 4

This is a light soup that works great for all dietary preferences. It feeds the vegetarians, vegans, gluten-free, and even dairy-free folks if you leave off the yogurt topping. It makes for a great dish to freeze and warm up when you're in need of some make-ahead meals. The trick to getting the lentils crispy is having them as dry as possible before adding them to the hot pan. I undercook the lentils just a bit, drain them well, and spread them on a dish towel while I make the soup to dry them out as much as possible before crisping them up. Don't even consider using canned here; they'll be a mushy mess.

A pureed soup like this can always be thinned to your liking with more broth or coconut milk. It thickens slightly as it cools, so make it a tad thinner than what you would like to enjoy when you sit down with your bowl and spoon.

2½ tablespoons coconut oil

1 yellow onion, coarsely chopped

1 teaspoon turmeric

3 tablespoons freshly grated ginger

2 teaspoon sweet curry powder

2 pounds peeled sweet potatoes (about 2 large), cut into 1-inch cubes

3 cups vegetable broth

½ cup orange juice

1 to 2 tablespoons Sriracha sauce

1 cup coconut milk

Sea salt and freshly ground pepper

1 large shallot

1¼ cups cooked black lentils, drained

Whole milk yogurt, for serving

1 bunch of fresh cilantro, coarsely chopped

⅓ cup toasted and chopped cashews, for serving

In a large pot, heat 1 tablespoon of the coconut oil over medium heat. Add the onion and sauté until translucent, about 2 minutes. Add the turmeric, ginger, and curry powder and give it another minute or two. Add the sweet potatoes and the broth to the pot. Bring the broth to a simmer, cover and cook for for 15 to 20 minutes until the sweet potatoes are cooked through. Add the orange juice, and use an immersion blender or regular blender to puree the soup. Stir in 1 tablespoon of the Sriracha, adding more to taste, and the coconut milk. Season with salt and pepper. Cover and keep the heat on low while you prepare the lentils.

Heat the remaining coconut oil over high heat. Mince the shallot. Add the shallot and lentils to the pan and fry for 2 minutes until crispy and hot.

Serve each bowl with a swirl of yogurt, spoonful of the lentils, fresh cilantro, and cashews.

Herbed Falafel Bowl

Serves 4

In a pita or on a salad, falafels are a great vegetarian meal. These are baked, not fried, and the usual bread crumbs are replaced with flax and nuts, which makes them slightly more delicate and grain free. Falafel are perfect to have on hand for lunches on the go. Even if they lose their shape tussled in your lunch box, the flavor is still great. I make a few suggestions for veggies to put in your bowl, but would work any number of things—pickled beets, shredded carrots, leftover roasted vegetables. I just use what's in the crisper.

Be sure to drain your beans well; excess water makes the falafel difficult to shape. If using canned beans, you'll notice a smoother texture and less water retention if you push the beans out of their skins before using.

FALAFEL

3 cloves garlic

½ teaspoon red pepper flakes

2 teaspoons cumin

½ teaspoon sea salt

½ teaspoon freshly ground pepper

1½ tablespoons extra-virgin olive oil

Zest of 1 lemon

2 teaspoons freshly squeezed lemon juice

2 Medjool dates, pitted

½ yellow onion

2 cups cooked and well-drained chickpeas

½ cup toasted pistachios

1 small bunch, chopped cilantro (about 1 cup)

⅓ cup coarsely chopped flat-leaf parsley

¼ cup coarsely chopped mint leaves

2 tablespoons flax seed meal

½ teaspoon baking soda

—

1 head romaine, finely shredded

1 English cucumber, sliced thin

1 pound tomatoes, sliced in wedges

Tahini Citrus Miso Dressing (page 203)

3 cups cooked brown rice, for serving

For the falafel, in the bowl of a food processor, add the garlic, pepper flakes, cumin, sea salt, pepper, olive oil, lemon zest and juice, dates, and onion. Process until well mixed. Add the chickpeas and pistachios and give it a few pulses until chunky; do not puree. Add the cilantro, parsley, mint, flax seed meal, and baking soda and pulse until the herbs are just incorporated. You want a coarse mixture, not too smooth. This can be done up to 2 days in advance and kept covered in the fridge.

Place a rack in the upper third of the oven and preheat to 375°F. Line a baking sheet with parchment paper. Rub a little oil on your hands, form 2-inch balls with the batter, and arrange them on the baking sheet; you'll have around 20. Brush a thin layer of olive oil on top. Bake 22 to 25 minutes, until the tops are browned.

Toss the romaine, cucumber, and tomatoes with the dressing. Serve each bowl with the rice, vegetables, and falafel.

Hippie Bowl

I use the word *hippie* with utmost endearment. I feel like sprouts, sunflower seeds, tofu, and avocado are all items that came from the original health food trends, and we are embracing them here in this light bowl meal. You can replace the millet with brown rice or the tofu for another protein if you prefer—this recipe takes well to substitutions. I'll also note that this meal packs well for plane trips and long car rides—nothing terribly perishable and it fills you up with all its fiber and crunch. It's Hugh's favorite bowl and his other favorite food is cheeseburgers, so that's enough for me.

¼ cup coconut sugar

3 tablespoons low-sodium soy sauce or tamari

3 tablespoons sambal oelek (chile paste)

1½ tablespoons apple cider vinegar

3 tablespoons toasted sesame oil

2 (14-ounce) extra packages firm tofu

—

SPICED SUNFLOWER SEEDS

¾ cup raw sunflower seeds

¼ teaspoon sea salt

¼ teaspoon cayenne

1 tablespoon muscovado sugar

—

1 cup millet

2 cups low-sodium vegetable broth

2 tablespoons extra-virgin olive oil or coconut oil

3 cloves garlic, minced

4 cups stemmed, chopped kale

4 cups (about 5 ounces) baby spinach

Sea salt

Juice of ½ lemon

4 carrots, shaved into ribbons

1 cup sprouts (broccoli, pea, or micro greens)

2 avocados, peeled and quartered

Tahini Citrus Miso Dressing (page 203)

In a shallow dish, whisk together the coconut sugar, soy sauce, sambal oelek, vinegar, and sesame oil. Drain and press the tofu between the layers of a folded dish-towel to absorb any excess liquid. Cut each block into 1-inch squares; toss them in the marinade and let soak for at least 30 minutes—a few hours is even better—flipping them halfway through. Preheat the oven to 475°F.

For the spiced sunflower seeds, heat a nonstick skillet over medium heat and toast the sunflower seeds until just fragrant, about 2 minutes. Add the salt, cayenne, and sugar and toss them around until the sugar is hot enough to stick to the seeds, 8 to 10 minutes. Transfer to a piece of parchment and spread out in a single layer to cool. The seeds can be made up to 3 days ahead and stored in an airtight container.

In a small pot over medium-low heat, add the millet and toast for a few minutes until you hear them start to pop. Add the broth, bring it to a boil, turn it down to a simmer and cover and cook for 15 to 18 minutes, until millet is tender. Turn off the heat, remove the lid, fluff with a fork, and stir in 1 tablespoon of the oil. Cover it again and let sit until ready to use.

Spread the tofu on a rimmed baking sheet lined with parchment; it's okay if some of the marinade drips. Bake for 20 to 25 minutes, tossing halfway through, until the edges are browned.

To sauté the greens, heat the remaining 1 tablespoon of olive oil over medium heat in a large skillet, add the garlic, and sauté until fragrant. Add the kale and spinach in batches with a pinch of salt and the lemon juice and sauté just until wilted, about 2 minutes.

Assemble your bowl with a portion of the millet, and then add your other toppings in quadrants on top: a scoop of tofu beside the warm greens, the carrot ribbons next to the sprouts. Top with some avocado, a hearty sprinkle of spiced sunflower seeds, and a generous drizzle of the tahini dressing.

Lentil *and* Mushroom Stuffed Peppers over Goat Cheese Butternut Mash

Serves 4

This plates as more of a layered bowl—a fluffy pillow of mashed squash with your stuffed pepper overflowing on top and some crunchy slaw on the side for contrast. I have served this to many non vegetarian dinner guests and no one misses the meat. It is warm, delicately spiced, and full of color.

I love this simple mash, but really don't like the fibery texture of winter squashes out of season. When you can't get your hands on a good squash, replace the butternut flesh with the insides of about three baked sweet potatoes. If you are unable to find poblanos, a small bell pepper will work fine as an alternative. Serve this with a side of crunchy lime-dressed cabbage slaw (I get a perfect, delicate shred on a mandoline or the slicer blade on a food processor) and you've got yourself a gorgeous vegetarian dinner.

SQUASH

1 large butternut squash (about 3 pounds)

1 tablespoon extra-virgin olive oil or coconut oil

Sea salt and freshly ground pepper

1 tablespoon maple syrup

¼ to ½ teaspoon cayenne pepper

1 teaspoon smoked paprika

5 ounces soft goat cheese (chevre), plus more for garnish

¼ cup whole milk or low sodium vegetable broth, as needed

—

SLAW

2 tablespoons sour cream

1 tablespoon pumpkin seed or grapeseed oil

Zest and juice of 2 limes

2 teaspoons natural cane sugar

Sea salt and freshly ground pepper

6 cups thinly shredded green cabbage, about ½ head

2 green onions, white and green parts, thinly sliced

½ cup chopped cilantro

—

PEPPERS AND FILLING

4 poblano peppers

3 tablespoons extra-virgin olive oil

½ yellow onion, coarsely chopped

½ teaspoon sea salt

1 pound cremini mushrooms, cleaned, stemmed and coarsely chopped

3 cloves garlic, minced

1½ cups cooked black or French green lentils

½ cup low-sodium vegetable broth

2 teaspoons cumin

1 tablespoon red wine vinegar

½ cup chopped cilantro, for garnish

½ cup toasted pepitas (pumpkin seeds), for garnish

For the squash, preheat the oven to 425°F. Cut the squash in half lengthwise and scoop out and discard the seeds. Rub the flesh with the oil, sprinkle with salt and pepper, and roast in the upper third of the oven, cut-side up, for 40 minutes, until blistered and soft throughout. Remove and set aside until cool to the touch.

Scoop the flesh into a large mixing bowl. Add the maple syrup, cayenne, paprika, goat cheese, and a pinch of salt and mash until smooth. Add a splash of milk only if you need more liquid to get it smooth. Set aside until ready to use.

For the slaw, in a large mixing bowl, whisk together the sour cream, oil, lime zest and juice, sugar, and a few pinches of salt and pepper and whisk together. Add the cabbage, green onions, and cilantro and toss everything to coat. Set aside until ready to serve; it benefits from sitting for 10 to 15 minutes.

For the peppers, cut a long slit in the peppers lengthwise and remove the ribs and seeds. Rub them with about 1 tablespoon of the oil and a sprinkle of salt. They can be cooked on a grill or grill pan, or roast the halves at 425°F in the upper third of the oven, for 12 to 15 minutes to just soften while you prepare the filling.

For the filling, in a large pan, heat 1 tablespoon of the oil over medium heat. Add the onions and salt and sauté until translucent. Add the mushrooms and continue to cook, stirring occasionally, allowing the mushrooms to release their liquid. When most of the water has evaporated, 6 to 8 minutes, add the remaining 1 tablespoon of the oil, the garlic, lentils, and broth and stir to mix. Simmer everything until warmed through. Stir in the cumin and vinegar.

Fill the poblanos with the lentil mixture—it's fine for some to spill over. Prepare each bowl with a portion of the squash pillowed on the bottom, topped with a stuffed pepper and a side of slaw. Garnish each bowl with a generous handful of cilantro, pepitas, and crumbled goat cheese.

Double-Pesto Zucchini Noodles

Serves 4

I have a tough time calling this recipe a "big bowl" because it's so light. You'll likely want to serve this with some garlic bread, and you could add grilled shrimp or chicken sausages if you're looking to bulk it up for the omnivores. The lentil "meatballs" in my first book would also be perfect here. I pack in a ton of flavor by making a quick pesto and then stirring in the components of pesto to finish the dish. I suggest five zucchini, assuming yours are a hearty size. If you have ones on the smaller side, shred up six or seven, so there's enough to go around.

Unlike most recipes here, the leftovers don't reheat well, so this is a dish you'll want to cook and eat the same day. It is even worth trying raw if the summer days are warm and a cool noodle dish sounds better—simply skip the sauté and dress the drained zucchini in pesto. The pesto may be prepared a few days in advance and any extra makes for an excellent sandwich spread or salad dressing when thinned with a little lemon juice.

---

5 large zucchini	1 pound vine-ripened tomatoes, stems attached
Sea salt	
—	2 tablespoons extra-virgin olive oil, as needed
PESTO	2 cloves garlic, minced
1 large clove garlic	1½ cups cooked white beans, rinsed and drained
¼ cup toasted pine nuts	
Juice of ½ lemon	Freshly ground pepper
½ teaspoon sea salt	⅓ cup toasted pine nuts
½ teaspoon freshly ground black pepper	1 cup basil, julienned
2 cups firmly packed basil	¾ cup shaved Parmesan
½ cup extra-virgin olive oil	Pinch of red pepper flakes
⅓ cup grated Parmesan cheese	Fresh lemon zest, for garnish

Preheat the oven to 425°F.

Using a julienne peeler, slice the zucchini into thin strips, stopping when you get to the seedy center. This can also be done with a spiral slicer, mandoline, or very carefully by hand. Lay the zucchini "noodles" on a dish towel and sprinkle them with sea salt; let them sweat for about 20 minutes, then blot and gently squeeze out the excess water with the dish towel.

Meanwhile, for the pesto, in a food processor, blend the garlic, pine nuts, lemon juice, salt, and pepper to a paste. Add the basil and blend to combine. With the

the sprouted kitchen bowl + spoon

motor running, add the olive oil, and then the Parmesan. Taste and adjust as needed (I like to add lots of lemon). Transfer to a jar and set aside.

Keeping stems attached, rub the tomatoes with a thin coat of oil and a sprinkle of salt and pepper. Roast them on a rimmed baking sheet for 10 to 12 minutes until they just begin to collapse.

In your largest frying pan over medium heat, warm the olive oil. Add the garlic and sauté for 1 minute until fragrant. Add the white beans, a hearty pinch of salt and pepper, and sauté just to warm through. Add the zucchini and gently sauté for 5 to 6 minutes until warmed (too long and they'll get soggy). Gently toss them in ⅓ cup of the prepared pesto (add more to taste) and half of the pine nuts, basil, and Parmesan.

Serve each bowl with a generous garnish of the remaining pine nuts, basil, Parmesan, pinch of red pepper flakes, and a fresh grate of lemon zest. Snip the tomatos at the stem into four portions and serve alongside the noodles.

Roasted Salmon, Haricots Verts, *and* Celeriac-Yukon Mash

Serves 4

Cooking salmon on a lower heat prevents healthy fats from seizing too quickly as they would in a quick, high heat sear. The result from this slow-cook is a more delicate texture; the fat melts into the flesh, giving you a very tender fish. I also like the method in this recipe for entertaining because I don't have to worry as much about overcooking the salmon. You have a slightly longer grace period than on a stove top or a grill. I can start the fish, finish up the green beans, toss together a simple salad, and am still able to keep my eye on the fish. If you are worried about the timing, err on the side of pulling it just before it is cooked through, as it will continue to cook as it rests.

I call for a small amount of cider here, which imparts just a subtle amount of sweetness to the mash. If you don't think you'll use the rest of the cider, a good vegetable or chicken stock will do. The green beans are light in flavor to contrast the mash, but a sprinkle of grated Parmesan never hurt anyone.

MASH

2 medium celeriac (celery root) (about 2 pounds)

2 to 3 Yukon gold potatoes (about 1½ pounds)

1 small yellow onion, peeled and coarsely diced

3 tablespoons unsalted butter

2 teaspoons whole grain mustard

⅓ cup apple cider

⅓ cup heavy cream

1 to 2 teaspoons sea salt

1 to 2 teaspoons freshly ground pepper

—

Zest of 1 lemon

3 tablespoons freshly squeezed lemon juice

3 teaspoons extra-virgin olive oil, divided

2 tablespoons minced shallot

2 teaspoons herbs de Provence

1½ pound wild salmon fillet

½ cup dry white wine

2 tablespoons finely chopped flat-leaf parsley

¾ pound haricots verts

1 small fennel bulb

⅓ cup toasted pine nuts

For the mash, peel the celeriac and cut it into 2-inch chunks. Peel the potatoes if you like, but that is only necessary if you're going for a silky smooth puree. Cut the potatoes into 2-inch chunks. Put the celeriac, potatoes, and onion in a large pot and cover them with water by 1 inch; add a few pinches of salt and bring to a boil. Turn the heat down to a simmer and cook for 25 to 30 minutes until tender; drain.

Continued

Using a ricer, food mill, or potato masher, mash the vegetables to a desired consistency. Add the butter, mustard, cider, cream, salt, and pepper and mash until mostly smooth. Season to taste with salt and pepper and add more liquid as needed; the puree will thicken as it sits. Cover and set aside.

Preheat the oven to 325°F and brush a large baking dish with olive oil. In a small bowl, combine the lemon zest, 2 tablespoons of the lemon juice, 1 tablespoon olive oil, shallot, and herbs de Provence and mix to combine. Lay the salmon fillet in the baking dish skin side down and season the fish well with sea salt. Spread the seasoning mixture on the flesh. Pour the white wine into the bottom of the dish; it's fine if it comes up the sides of the fish a bit. Bake on the middle rack for about 20 minutes until just opaque in the center. Cooking time may vary, 5 to 10 minutes depending on the size of the fish. Sprinkle the fish with the parsley when it's out of the oven.

While the fish bakes, steam the haricots verts until al dente, about 4 minutes. Shave the fennel paper thin. In a bowl, toss the beans and fennel with the remaining olive oil, the remaining lemon juice, the pine nuts, and a pinch of salt and pepper.

Serve each bowl with a scoop of the mash along with a portion of salmon and green beans.

Seared Scallops in Thai Broth

Serves 4

This bowl of seared scallops in a fragrant Thai broth gets its unique freshness from lemongrass, and heat from the ginger and chiles. The scallops are served with the accompaniments added as you wish—rice to tame the spice, and some sweet fruit to complement it. Seek out fresh scallops if you can as they don't retain water the way the previously frozen ones do; pat them dry and they will give you a nice crust when you sear them. Other mild fish, or tofu will also work.

I like a subtle amount of heat—the sort that warms your mouth but doesn't make you feel like you may be on fire. For the broth, I remove all the ribs and seeds from the red chile and still get plenty of warmth. If you're one for sweaty palms, leave a couple of seeds in; if not, use half of the ribbed and seeded chile. It's always easier to add heat than take it away.

BROTH

2 teaspoons coconut oil

2 stalks lemongrass, tough ends and outer leaves removed

1 (1-inch) piece of fresh ginger or galangal

2 cloves garlic, minced

1 small red Thai chile, ribs and seeds completely removed, chopped

½ teaspoon sea salt

1 (14-ounce) can coconut milk

1½ cups low-sodium vegetable broth

1 tablespoon fish sauce (optional)

1 cup jasmine rice (or 2¼ cups cooked)

—

SALAD

1 red bell pepper, ribs and seeds removed

1 mango

3 green onions

8 ounces hearts of palm, drained

1 teaspoon toasted sesame oil

Zest and juice of 1 lime

Sea salt and freshly ground pepper

1 cup coarsely chopped cilantro

—

12 jumbo scallops

2 tablespoons coconut oil

1 cup roasted and salted peanuts, coarsely chopped

For the broth, in a Dutch oven or large pot, heat the coconut oil over medium heat. Coarsely chop the lemongrass, hitting it a few times with the side of a knife to release the oils. Add the lemongrass to the pot. Peel and grate the ginger and add it, the garlic, chile, and salt to the pot and sauté until fragrant and softened, about 2 minutes. Add the coconut milk, vegetable broth, and fish sauce and bring to a simmer. Turn the heat to low and let everything steep for 15 minutes. This can be done a day in advance.

Continued

To mix, run an immersion blender through the pot to break up the large pieces, or blend it in a blender or food processor. Strain the broth through a fine-mesh strainer back into the pot to remove the solids. Season to taste with salt and pepper. Keep covered on very low heat to keep warm.

Rinse the rice and cook according to package instructions.

For the mango salad, slice the bell pepper and mango into thin slices and put them in a mixing bowl. Slice the green onions and hearts of palm thinly on a diagonal and add to the bowl. Add the sesame oil, lime zest and juice, a hearty pinch of salt and freshly ground pepper, and cilantro and toss everything to coat. The mango salad can be made a day in advance.

Pat the scallops dry. Sprinkle all sides with salt and pepper. In a large skillet, heat the coconut oil over medium-high heat. When the oil is shimmering, add the scallops and sear, without touching them, for 2 minutes on each side. The flesh will start to pull away from the pan after 2 minutes, making them easier to flip.

Put two ladlefuls of the broth into serving bowls. Add a scoop of rice, scallops, and top with the mango salad and peanuts with any extras served on the side.

Smoky Black Bean Chili

Serves 6

This soup is my answer to having more than one other couple over for dinner without expending more than moderate effort and an inexpensive grocery run. I play the casual card and serve big bowls of this with all the toppings on the side along with a warm cast-iron pan of cornbread. The recipe feeds six people well with likely a bit left over. I suppose you could use canned beans in a pinch, but soaking and cooking the beans from scratch yields a really fresh-tasting bean—it's a completely different texture. I am including the steps to cook the beans; if you are using canned, you'll need to add about 6 cups (about 3 cans—2 black, 1 kidney). There are a lot of spices, but not a long list of ingredients, so cooking your own beans is a worthwhile step. I also highly recommend a creamy addition for serving, be it avocado, cheese, or sour cream. The soup is extremely low fat. It needs that rich hit at the end. This is a sturdy chili; add broth if you prefer it thinner, or run an immersion blender through the pot if you like more viscosity. The whole thing can be made a day or two in advance, so it's a great meal when you need to prep ahead of time.

½ pound dry black beans

½ pound dry kidney beans

2 bay leaves

1 tablespoon grapeseed oil or ghee

1 large yellow onion, diced

1 red bell pepper, diced

5 cloves garlic, minced

2 teaspoons cumin

2 teaspoons dried oregano

2 teaspoons smoked paprika

1 tablespoon cocoa powder

2 tablespoons chili powder

¼ teaspoon chipotle powder

3 to 4 cups low-sodium vegetable broth

1 (28-ounce) can diced tomatoes, or 1½ pounds fresh, diced

1 tablespoon tomato paste

¾ cup cooked brown rice

1 tablespoon apple cider vinegar

Cilantro, avocado, and sour cream, for garnish

Sea salt and freshly ground pepper

Pick through the beans, then rinse them well. In a large bowl, cover them generously with water, and soak overnight on the counter. The next day, drain the beans and transfer to a large pot. Cover them with fresh water by a couple of inches and bring them to a boil with the bay leaves. Lower the heat to a simmer and cook the beans for 1 to 1½ hours, until cooked through. Stir in a pinch of salt at the end and set aside.

Meanwhile, prepare the rest of the ingredients. Heat the oil in a large pot and sauté the onion over medium heat until softened, about 3 minutes. Add the bell pepper, garlic, ½ teaspoon salt, cumin, oregano, paprika, cocoa powder, chili powder, chipotle powder and cook 5 minutes longer. Add 3 cups of the broth, the tomatoes, tomato paste, and the chipotle chili and simmer for 15 minutes. Drain the beans of excess water and add them to the onion mixture. Add the rice, stir, and simmer on low for 10 minutes longer. Season to taste with the vinegar, additional broth, salt, or spice, if needed.

Garnish each serving with cilantro, avocado, and sour cream, and as you wish. Chili will keep covered in the fridge for 1 week.

Tahini Kale Slaw *and* Roasted Tamari Portobello Bowl

Serves 2

I have been working as a personal chef for a couple who have a handful of dietary preferences. While it can be a challenge to think twice before I prepare meals, I'm usually surprised with how delicious things can be without the heaviness of wheat, dairy, and meat. It's a reminder to rise to the occasion, I suppose. Tamari is a wheat-free version of soy sauce, but either can work here if you don't have an issue with wheat. This bowl is one I now make repeatedly for my own family and a great option for people with vegetarian, vegan, dairy- or gluten-free eating habits. If you're serving more than two, assume one portobello per person and multiply from there.

2 large portobello mushrooms

2 tablespoons toasted sesame or grapeseed oil

Sea salt and fresh ground pepper

1 tablespoon tamari or low sodium soy sauce

—

SLAW

1 bunch lacinato kale, stems removed

1 carrot, grated

3 green onions, white and green parts, chopped

Tahini Citrus Miso Dressing (page 203)

½ cup sunflower sprouts or microgreens

—

1 cup cooked brown rice

1 large avocado, peeled and diced

⅓ cup roasted and salted sunflower seeds

Preheat the oven to 375°F and line a baking sheet with parchment or foil. Remove the stems from the mushrooms and rub both sides with the oil and a sprinkle of sea salt and pepper. Place them gill side up on the baking sheet and drizzle the tamari on top. Roast for 15 to 18 minutes until the mushrooms look soft and collapsed. Once cool, slice them thinly.

While the mushrooms cook, prepare the slaw. Finely chop the kale. In a large mixing bowl, combine the kale, shredded carrots, green onions and dress as desired. Rub the dressing into the kale to soften it and then add the sprouts.

Serve each bowl, warm or cold, with a good portion of the kale, scoop of rice, a mushroom, avocado, and a generous sprinkle of sunflower seeds.

Spring Noodles *with* Artichokes, Pecorino, *and* Charred Lemons

Serves 4

Artichokes, in all their naturally creamy and slightly earthy glory, can be included a few ways here. Steaming and paring down a few fresh ones to get a collection of tender hearts is a job for a slow Sunday with extra time. On an average weeknight, I use frozen or jarred (I like the marinated ones), which work just fine here and will take you much less time to prepare. The char on the lemons takes the bitterness out of the rind and gives you a subtly tart bite. They do still contribute a bold flavor, so be sure to chop your pieces small.

I have the egg in here to add viscosity to the sauce, like a traditional Italian pasta carbonara. It's not crucial if you prefer to leave it out, but it makes for a nice coating on the noodles. When I say "large sauté pan," I really mean large, as you'll be tossing everything together in there. Use a Dutch oven or toss everything back into the pasta pot if you need more space.

---

2 small Meyer lemons

2 teaspoons extra-virgin olive oil

1 teaspoon natural cane sugar

—

4 tablespoons unsalted butter, divided

2 endives, trimmed

3 cloves garlic, minced

1 (14-ounce) can, 1 (12-ounce) frozen package, or 3 large, fresh steamed artichoke hearts, chopped

Sea salt and freshly ground pepper

3 tablespoons white balsamic vinegar

½ cup plus 2 tablespoons crème fraîche

¼ teaspoon freshly grated nutmeg

½ teaspoon cayenne

1 teaspoon dried Italian herbs

12 ounces (¾ pound) fusilli or shell pasta

1 egg, at room temperature

1¼ cups coarsely grated pecorino cheese

2 to 3 cups arugula

Fresh parsley, for garnish

Fresh dill, for garnish

Slice the lemons crosswise into ¼-inch rings and remove the seeds with a small knife. Toss the slices with the olive oil and sugar. Grill or broil the slices, flipping halfway through, until char marks appear on the lemons and they begin to soften. Set aside.

Bring a stock pot of salted water to a boil.

In a large sauté pan over medium heat, melt 2 tablespoons of the butter. Slice the endive lengthwise, discarding the tough core, and then into ½-inch half moons. Add the garlic and endives to the warm butter and sauté for 1 minute, just until softened. Add the artichoke hearts and a few pinches of salt and sauté until warmed. Stir in the remaining butter, white balsamic, crème fraîche, nutmeg,

cayenne, and dried herbs. Chop the lemons into small pieces and add them to the pan as well. Keep the heat on low and cover.

Cook the noodles according to package instructions. Drain and reserve ½ cup of the pasta water. In a small bowl, whisk the egg with ½ cup of the cheese and ¼ cup of the reserved pasta water. Into the vegetable mixture, add the noodles and egg mixture and toss until everything is coated and creamy, about 1 minute. Add the arugula and a few more pinches of salt and pepper to taste. Toss to mix, adding pasta water as needed to loosen the sauce.

Serve each bowl warm with a generous sprinkle of cheese and the fresh herbs.

Strawberry Tabbouleh

Albeit a good amount of chopping, this is my favorite dish to bring to picnics. It's easy to eat with all the ingredients chopped small and holds up well if it needs to travel or be made a day in advance.

For those avoiding gluten, quinoa can be substituted for the bulgur. If strawberries are out of season, roasted beets are a nice change and available year-round. I offer feta as an optional ingredient to not completely bastardize traditional tabbouleh, but my resident taste tester would argue it's absolutely necessary.

¾ cup bulgur wheat

1 clove garlic, finely minced

3 green onions, white and light green parts

1 pint strawberries

2 to 3 Persian cucumbers, or 1 English cucumber

⅓ cup finely chopped mint leaves

½ cup finely chopped flat-leaf parsley

¼up extra-virgin olive oil

1 tablespoon red wine vinegar

Zest and juice of 1 small lemon

½ to ¾ teaspoon sea salt

1 teaspoon freshly ground pepper

½ cup crumbled sheep milk feta (optional)

Rinse and drain the bulgur. Bring 1¼ cups water to a boil, add the bulgur, turn off the heat, cover and set aside for 25 to 30 minutes or until the liquid is absorbed. Stir in the garlic, fluff with a fork, and set aside to cool.

Thinly slice the green onions and add them to a large mixing bowl. Finely dice the strawberries and cucumbers and add them to the bowl. Add the cooled bulgur, mint, parsley, olive oil, vinegar, lemon zest and juice, salt, pepper, and feta and stir everything to mix well. Taste for seasonings and serve chilled or at room temperature.

The tabbouleh will keep, covered, in the fridge for 3 days, but it's best the day it's made.

Herby Leek *and* Pea Soup *with* Grainy Croutons

Serves 4

I enjoy light spring dinners as the weather teeters toward warm with a bit of chill still in the air. It begins to stay light longer and you have the excuse to sit at a table outside and phase out the comfort foods that sounded so delicious in the colder months. This soup sings of spring with its bright color, the nuanced onion flavor of leeks, and a hint of creaminess. The crispy croutons offer just enough crunch and substance, but a simple grilled cheese of rye bread and white Cheddar makes for a nice accompaniment as well.

3 large leeks, cleaned, dark green parts removed

2 tablespoons unsalted butter or ghee

Sea salt

4 cups low sodium vegetable broth

3 cups shelled peas, fresh or frozen

2 tablespoons each chopped tarragon, oregano, and parsley, plus more for garnish

½ teaspoon freshly ground pepper

⅓ cup crème fraîche

Juice of ½ lemon

½ loaf day-old rye or other grainy bread

2 tablespoons extra-virgin olive oil

Freshly grated Parmesan cheese (optional)

Slice the leeks into thin half circles.

In a large, heavy pot, melt the butter over medium heat. Add the leeks and a few pinches of salt and sauté until softened and cooked down to half their volume, 6 to 8 minutes. Add the broth, bring it to a simmer, and cook another 10 minutes. Add the peas, herbs, and pepper and cook 2 minutes longer. With an immersion blender, regular blender, or food processor, puree the soup until smooth. Stir in the crème fraîche and lemon juice to taste. Taste for salt and pepper and cover to keep warm.

Preheat the oven or toaster oven to 400°F. Rip the bread into 1-inch pieces, including crust; you'll want about 3 cups. Spread the oil on the baking sheet with a few pinches of salt and pepper and toss the pieces to coat. Spread the croutons in an even layer and bake for 10 to 12 minutes, stirring halfway through, or until the edges are just browned. Set aside to cool and crisp up.

Serve each bowl of soup with a handful of the croutons, a generous sprinkle of Parmesan, and the fresh tarragon, oregano, and parsley.

Summer Quinoa Salad

In the summer, I try not to spend as much time in the kitchen prepping, and lean toward meals that are quick and light. The goal is to make a few things in bulk that will keep for a few days and that I can throw together for easy meals. This salad packs up well for beach days or picnics, and is just as great with a couple of fried eggs on top for brunch. The simplicity beckons you to use fresh summer corn and tomatoes. While it's a simple crowd-pleasing (vegetarian, gluten free) dish for dinner al fresco with friends, the fact that both the quinoa and kale can hold up dressed for a few days make it a lovely dish to keep on hand for quick meals.

I use a 1 to 1.5 ratio of quinoa to water here because I like it on the al dente side for salads. This leaves you with individual grains as opposed to mush. If you find yours in need of a bit more liquid, just add a couple more tablespoons. I bake the tomatoes to hover somewhere between oven dried and fresh. I like the bits of juice and also the concentrated sweetness that the oven imparts to these summer gems. Leave them raw if you're in a hurry, but they make the salad special if you have the time.

½ cup quinoa (or 1 cup cooked and cooled quinoa)

¾ cup of water or broth

¾ pound cherry tomatoes

1 tablespoon extra-virgin olive oil

Sea salt and freshly ground pepper, to taste

1¼ cups corn kernels, from 2 small ears of corn

2½ cups stemmed, finely chopped kale

¾ cup chopped cilantro

⅓ cup toasted pine nuts

½ cup crumbled ricotta salata or feta cheese

—

DRESSING

2 cloves garlic

2 teaspoon Dijon mustard

2 tablespoons rice wine vinegar

3 tablespoons extra-virgin olive oil

¼ cup buttermilk

Sea salt and freshly ground pepper

Rinse and drain the quinoa. Put it in a pot with the water. Bring it to a simmer, cover, and cook for 15 minutes. Fluff it with a fork, turn off the heat, set the cover ajar, and set aside to cool completely.

Place a rack in the upper third of the oven and preheat to 325°F. Halve the tomatoes and spread them on a parchment lined, rimmed baking sheet. Drizzle on ½ tablespoon of the olive oil, a pinch of salt and pepper, and toss everything to coat. Spread the tomatoes in an even layer and roast for 30 to 35 minutes until slightly dried at the edges. Remove to cool.

Heat the remaining olive oil in a large frying pan over medium-high heat. Add the corn kernels and sauté, only stirring once or twice, for 2 minutes to just char the outside. Set aside to cool. Both of these steps may be done 1 day in advance.

In a large mixing bowl, combine the cooled quinoa, kale, and cilantro. When the tomatoes and corn are completely cool, add them along with the pine nuts and cheese to the bowl.

For the dressing, in a food processor or with a mortar and pestle, pulse or smash the garlic cloves. Add the mustard, vinegar, olive oil, buttermilk, and a hearty pinch of salt and pepper and mix everything to combine.

Toss the salad with the desired amount of dressing. This salad will keep, covered, in the fridge for 3 days.

Smoky Tortilla Soup

Serves 4

This is a soup I can typically throw together with things I keep in my pantry and fridge. It usually happens in the months when I can get excellent tomatoes, as their natural sweetness plays perfectly off the spice of the chiles. It looks plain and unassuming at first, but once everything is blended and toppings are on, it makes a much more satisfying bowl than your average brothy tortilla soup. Plus, it's easy to make, great for a weeknight, and the leftovers are even better. I'm including an option for chicken or beans, which I'm aware don't taste the same, because I want to encourage omnivore and vegetarian alike to make this soup. Each bowl can be topped with the protein of choice—ideal for a table of mixed eaters. I know the addition of butter in the soup sounds a bit luxe, but it makes the soup smooth and curiously creamy. I suppose you could go without, but I don't suggest it. And you must have the garnishes; tortilla soup garnishes are not optional.

---

2 medium dried ancho chiles

1 tablespoon extra-virgin olive oil

1 yellow onion, coarsely chopped

4 cloves garlic

Sea salt and freshly ground pepper

2 pounds tomatoes (beefsteak, Roma, or a mix)

1 chipotle chile in adobo, or ¼ teaspoon chipotle powder

4 to 5 cups low-sodium vegetable or chicken stock

2 tablespoons unsalted butter

4 tablespoons cornmeal or finely ground polenta

2 cups finely shredded chicken and/or pinto beans

Cilantro, avocado, Cotija cheese, and tortilla chips, for garnish

---

Soak the ancho chiles in hot water for 20 minutes. Remove and discard stem and seeds. Heat the olive oil in a large pot or saucepan over medium heat. Add the onion and garlic with a large pinch of salt and sauté until softened, about 5 minutes. Halve the tomatoes, discard some of the seeds if they're easy to remove, and add them to the pot along with the chiles, chipotle, and 4 cups of the stock. Turn the heat down slightly, let the stock come to a gentle simmer, and cook for about 30 minutes, until everything is softened.

With an immersion blender, or in batches in a standard blender, puree the soup until smooth. Stir in the butter and cornmeal and simmer 5 to 8 minutes longer for the cornmeal to thicken the soup. Add more broth, as needed, for desired texture. Taste and season with salt and pepper. Soup can be made up to 2 days ahead and kept covered in the fridge.

Prepare your garnishes and top each bowl with chicken or pinto beans and generous handfuls of chopped cilantro, avocado, Cotija, and crispy tortilla chips.

Turkey Meatballs in Tomato Sauce

Serves 4

These are the sort of meatballs just to serve on their own in a simple tomato sauce, along with wedges of warm garlic bread and a giant salad. They are tender and flavorful and enjoyed simply with a bowl and spoon, pushed along with that crusty bread. I braise these in tomatoes and wine, but I'll use marinara when I want a little more depth of flavor, especially if they're heading on top of noodles.

Hugh's answer, when I ask what to change about a recipe, is usually to add bacon. You'll have to trust him here, as the lean turkey really benefits from the salty and savory bits of bacon, which are your luxury in this lighter turkey version. I am not including bacon in the recipe as it works fine without it, but my head recipe critic suggests 3 pieces of cooked bacon, chopped and stirred into the turkey mixture. Take it or leave it.

MEATBALLS

½ cup ricotta cheese

2 tablespoons milk

⅓ cup grated Parmesan, plus more for garnish

1 egg, beaten

3 cloves garlic, minced

2 teaspoons fennel seeds

2 teaspoons dried oregano

½ teaspoon red pepper flakes

½ teaspoon smoked salt or sea salt

¼ teaspoon freshly ground pepper

⅓ cup minced red onion

¼ cup chopped flat-leaf parsley

2 pieces whole grain bread, crust removed, or ⅔ cup panko (Japanese bread crumbs)

1 pound ground turkey (not fat free)

—

SAUCE

1 (28-ounce) can crushed tomatoes

¼ cup red wine

2 tablespoons melted unsalted butter

½ teaspoon salt

Chopped fresh parsley and basil, for garnish

In a large mixing bowl, combine the ricotta, milk, Parmesan, egg, and garlic and stir well to mix. Put the fennel seeds, oregano, red pepper flakes, and smoked salt in a pile on a cutting board and chop the spices to coarsely smash and grind up the fennel seeds. Add the spice mixture, pepper, onion, and parsley to the ricotta mixture and stir to combine. Rip the bread into small pieces and stir it into the ricotta mixture to saturate. Allow to sit for 10 minutes so the bread becomes moist, and then smash everything with the back of a fork to mix. Add the turkey meat (and bacon if using) and gently mix the meat into the wet mixture until just combined, being careful not to overmix. Cover and let the mixture rest for at least 30 minutes; this much can be done a day in advance and kept covered in the fridge.

Place a rack in the upper third of the oven and preheat to 400°F. Coat the bottom of a roasting pan or large, ovenproof baking dish with olive oil. Roll the meat mixture into 1½-inch balls and place them in the prepared dish, 1 inch apart. Roast the meatballs for 15 minutes to brown the edges.

Meanwhile, for the sauce, put the tomatoes in a bowl and crush them with your hands to make a sauce. Stir in the wine, melted butter, and salt.

Remove the meatballs from the oven and turn down the heat to 325°F. Pour the tomato mixture over the meatballs, cover the pan with foil, and return to the oven for 20 to 25 minutes to cook through.

Serve the warm meatballs with a good scoop of the sauce. Garnish each bowl generously with freshly grated Parmesan, parsley, and basil.

Cauliflower Gratin

Serves 4

While I was pregnant, my eating habits changed despite my best efforts. I really wanted to crave salads, but bean and cheese burritos, french fries, pizza toast—basically any warm starch—were what usually sounded good. If I wanted to eat vegetables, they needed to be under the guise of a cheesy carb, so I baked up this cauliflower, in a lighter cheese sauce, to fool only myself. Still a far cry from a salad, this casserole is just the thing for a cold night in. You can add a cup of white beans or shredded chicken to make it more filling; you just need to double the sauce quantity so it doesn't dry out. The bread crumbs are optional. It's lovely with just the shredded cheese, but if you like a more crisp topping, adding panko to the cheese creates more of a crust—if we're going to drape our veggies in cheese sauce, let's just do it right, no?

2 pounds cauliflower florets	¼ teaspoon cayenne
1 cup cooked brown rice	½ teaspoon dried Italian herbs
2 tablespoons unsalted butter	½ cup grated Parmesan, plus ¼ cup for topping
2 large cloves garlic, minced	¾ cup shredded Gruyère, plus ¼ cup for topping
¼ red onion, minced	
½ teaspoon sea salt	½ cup panko (Japanese bread crumbs), optional
½ teaspoon freshly ground pepper	
2 tablespoons unbleached all-purpose flour	2 teaspoons extra-virgin olive oil
	Freshly ground pepper
1½ cups milk, at room temperature	Chopped fresh parsley, for garnish
¼ teaspoon freshly grated nutmeg	

Place a rack in the middle of the oven and preheat to 400°F. Grease an 8-inch square pan.

Cut the cauliflower into bite-size pieces and steam for 5 to 7 minutes. Combine the cauliflower and brown rice in a mixing bowl and set aside.

In a saucepan, warm the butter over medium heat. Add the garlic, onion, salt, and pepper. Sauté until softened. Add the flour and cook 1 minute longer. Slowly start adding the milk, stirring to combine. Turn the heat down to low and let thicken. Add the nutmeg, cayenne, and Italian herbs. Stir in the Parmesan and Gruyère just until melted. Pour the warm cheese mixture over the cauliflower and rice, add another few pinches of salt and pepper, and stir to combine. Pour into the baking dish. Mix together the grated Gruyere, Parmesan, panko, olive oil, and pepper and sprinkle it on top. Bake for 20 minutes, or until the edges start to bubble. Turn the heat up to 500°F and cook 6 to 10 minutes, until the top is golden brown. Remove and let cool slightly. Sprinkle the top with parsley and serve warm.

SWEET BOWLS

An exquisite dessert in a restaurant appears stunning on a plate, but I find desserts in a bowl a bit more practical and fun to eat. And anything à la mode benefits from the side of a bowl to scoop against for gathering the perfect ratio of ice cream to crisp, for example. The recipes in this chapter are good for comfort classics for a crowd, like the **Gingered Apple Crisp** (page 160); lighter options for a girls' night, such as the **Key Lime Eton Mess** (page 172); or balmy evening barbeques, like for the **Cocoa Nib Pavlovas** (page 164).

Alternative natural sweeteners such as maple syrup, brown rice syrup, and extra-ripe bananas make their way into this collection of desserts in an attempt to keep moments of decadence slightly more wholesome; these ingredients can also offer more depth of flavor. But the truth of the matter is, it's a treat, so enjoy a sweet bowl for what it is.

Gingered Apple Crisp

A warm bowl after a holiday dinner, or a sweet breakfast of leftovers with a dollop of plain yogurt; there is nothing particularly new about an apple crisp, but it's one of those things you just want a go-to recipe for. This one is a tender mixture of apples, and a crust that has both crunchy and cakey bits with flecks of pecan and teensy spicy ginger bits. The crisp topping may be prepared in advance to save time and the apple crisp assembled when needed. Especially if using cast iron, the pan retains heat, so even after you pull the crisp out, it will continue to cook. Just keep an eye on it; it's always safer to err on the side of too early than too late with a crisp. To make the topping gluten-free, replace the flour with oat flour and almond meal.

---

7 medium apples (Granny Smith, Braeburn, Pink Lady)

Zest and juice of 1 small lemon

2 tablespoons muscovado sugar

¼ teaspoon freshly grated nutmeg

½ teaspoon cinnamon

2 tablespoons white whole wheat flour

Sea salt

—

TOPPING

3 to 4 tablespoons chopped crystallized ginger

¾ cup muscovado sugar (or natural cane sugar)

1 cup white whole wheat flour

½ cup old-fashioned oats

⅔ cup chopped pecan pieces

½ teaspoon sea salt

1 teaspoon cinnamon

3 tablespoons honey

1 teaspoon pure vanilla extract

½ cup unsalted butter, at room temperature

—

Ice cream or whipped cream, for serving

Lightly butter a 12-inch ovenproof skillet or baking dish. Place a rack in the middle of the oven and preheat to 375°F.

Peel and core the apples and cut them into 2-inch cubes. In a large mixing bowl, combine the apples with the lemon zest and juice, sugar, nutmeg, cinnamon, flour, and a pinch of sea salt and toss to coat. Transfer to the skillet.

For the topping, in the same mixing bowl, add the crystallized ginger, sugar, flour, oats, pecans, salt, and cinnamon and give it a stir to mix. Add the honey, vanilla, and butter and work it in with your fingers until everything is evenly coated. It will look like chunky, damp sand. Spread the topping evenly over the apples and bake for 25 to 30 minutes, or until the top is browned and the apples, still have resistance to them.

Let the crisp cool for at least 10 minutes before serving with a scoop of ice cream.

Chai-Spiced Brown Rice Pudding

Serves 4

It was not until I began working at a grocery store that I realized how many people really enjoy rice pudding. In an effort to offer a dairy and gluten-free option, I played around with lots of spices to give this creamy bowl an interesting flair. If you prefer to avoid eggs, this can be made without; it will just be slightly less rich and have an oatmeal consistency instead of pudding. I use coconut sugar for its deep caramel flavor, but muscovado or brown sugar will stand in just fine.

½ cup medium-grain brown rice

1 cup brewed black tea

1 cup water

1 (14-ounce) can whole or light coconut milk

1 egg

¼ cup coconut sugar

¼ cup natural cane sugar

1 vanilla bean, or ½ teaspoon pure vanilla extract

¼ teaspoon ground cardamom

¼ teaspoon cinnamon, plus more for garnish

¼ teaspoon crushed pink peppercorns

1 teaspoon freshly grated ginger

Toasted chopped almonds, for garnish

In a saucepan over medium heat, combine the rice, tea, water, and a pinch of salt. Bring it up to a boil, stirring occasionally, then down to a simmer, cover and cook for 25 minutes. Uncover, stir in the coconut milk, and continue to simmer, stirring frequently, until the rice is tender and the liquid has reduced, about 10 minutes. Turn the heat to the lowest setting.

Beat the egg, sugars, vanilla seeds, cardamom, cinnamon, peppercorns, and ginger together. Turn off the heat and slowly stir the egg mixture into the warm pudding. Continue to stir vigorously to incorporate, scraping the bottom to keep the egg from curdling, for 1 minute longer until the steam subsides. It will still be quite loose; the pudding will tighten as it sits.

Garnish with a dash of cinnamon and a sprinkle of almonds. Serve warm or chilled.

Cocoa Nib Pavlovas *with* Mixed Berries

Makes 8 to 12

I used to nanny for a family whose mom was from New Zealand. Both New Zealand and Australian folks are patriotic about their pavlovas; it's what pie is to the United States—part of our food culture. She taught me about pavlovas and made a stunning one anytime company came over. They make for a delightful dessert. I use the French method for meringue here; it doesn't heat the egg whites first, so there is some texture from the natural sugars, which I actually prefer. These are truly a treat that don't weigh you down after a meal, naturally gluten free, and a step away from dairy free if you choose to replace the heavy cream with a whipped coconut cream. The bowl element here is that I make a well in each pavlova before baking that will get filled with cream and fruit when served. That "bowl" can be filled with a fruit curd, chocolate ganache, raspberry coulis, or even some pomegrante seeds in the winter months. You can take the pavlova in so many directions. Plan to make the meringues 1 day in advance, or at least 6 hours before they're needed, so they can completely cool and crisp up.

---

4 egg whites, at room temperature

¾ cup natural cane sugar

¼ cup muscovado sugar

½ teaspoon pure vanilla extract

2 tablespoons cocoa nibs

Pinch of salt

—

FILLING

2 cups (1 pint) light whipping cream

2 tablespoons natural cane sugar or confectioners' sugar

½ teaspoon pure vanilla extract

4 cups mixed berries, fresh or frozen, thawed

1 tablespoon maple syrup (optional)

Preheat the oven to 210°F and line a large rimmed baking sheet with parchment paper.

In a stand mixer, add the egg whites and whisk on medium-high until you get glossy, soft peaks, about 6 to 8 minutes. In two additions, add both sugars, the salt, and continue to beat to incorporate. When the peaks are almost stiff, add the vanilla and cocoa nibs and and whisk the mixture one more time to incorporate. The meringue should look pillowy but stabilized.

On the parchment-lined baking sheet, divide the mixture into 8 meringue pillows, or 12 smaller portions, depending on the size you prefer. Use the back of a spoon to create a generous well in the middle so the edges are higher than the center. Bake the meringues for 50 to 60 minutes, until dried. They will brown a bit due to the natural sugars. Turn off the heat and allow them to cool completely in the oven.

You can make the meringues up to 2 days in advance and keep them in an airtight container until ready to use.

For the filling, whip the cream with the sugar and vanilla until soft peaks form. Clean and collect the berries in a large mixing bowl; toss with the maple syrup, if your berries are not very sweet.

Prepare each pavlova with one meringue, a helping of the whipped cream, and a scoop of fresh berries on top. Once assembled, enjoy the pavlova within an hour, before the meringue begins to disintegrate under the cream.

Coconut Sorbet *with* Strawberry Rhubarb Sauce

Serves 6

Every "sweets person" has his or her weakness, the sweet above all other sweets. Mine is ice cream. I can turn down candy, pie, a birthday cake, but I am forever faithful to ice cream. I prefer my treats frozen, warm, or a contrast of both—fresh ice cream cookie sandwiches! A la mode anything! Recently, I started experimenting with coconut milk-based ice creams and sorbets, and I honestly don't believe much is compromised. The texture is slightly different, but it's hardly a sacrifice. Coconut milk has a high fat content just like cream, so you get the same silky richness. That said, after it's frozen, you'll want to let the sorbet sit for about 5 minutes to soften before scooping. Using coconut sugar will offer a brown hue to the sorbet and natural cane sugar will leave it white. The sauce here is almost like a loose jam, so whatever you don't use for sundaes, you can spread on toast or waffles.

---

3 cups coconut milk (about 2 13-ounce cans)

⅔ cup coconut sugar (or natural cane sugar)

1 tablespoon brown rice syrup

Sea salt

½ teaspoon pure vanilla extract

1½ tablespoons cornstarch

—

SAUCE

4 cups chopped ripe strawberries

¾ cup diced rhubarb

¼ cup natural cane sugar or coconut sugar

½ tablespoon freshly grated ginger (optional)

½ cup pistachios, very finely chopped

In a medium pot, warm 2 cups of the coconut milk, the sugar, brown rice syrup, and a pinch of salt. Simmer, stirring occasionally over medium heat until the sugar is dissolved. In a large bowl, add the remaining cup of coconut milk and stir in the vanilla and cornstarch to dissolve. Slowly stir the warm coconut milk into the coconut-cornstarch mixture. Set the bowl in the fridge to cool completely. Once cooled, churn the mixture in your ice cream maker according to the manufacturer's instructions. Leave the mixture to set fully in the freezer.

For the sauce, in a heavy saucepan over medium low heat, combine the strawberries, rhubarb, a pinch of salt, and the sugar. Leave everything to very gently simmer for about 20 minutes. Give it a stir and barely simmer again, stirring occasionally, for 10 minutes longer. You will have chunks of fruit between a loose liquid; this will set more as it cools to become a thicker sauce. Turn off the heat and stir in the ginger. Allow the mixture to cool, uncovered, to room temperature. The sauce can be kept, covered, in the fridge for 1 week.

Serve the sundaes with a puddle of the sauce, a few scoops of sorbet, another drizzle of sauce, and pistachios on top.

Double Chocolate Pudding

Serves 4 to 6

Everything I associate with pudding brings me back to Handi-Snacks and Jello packs from my childhood. These lunchbox memories don't ring "real food" for me, but this pudding, a simple homemade version, is rich and decadent and made of recognizable ingredients—plus it's a much easier process than you'd expect.

The coffee here only enhances the chocolate flavor; it doesn't make it taste like a mocha. I serve the pudding in small portions (quite precious in half-pint mason jars) with a dollop of fresh whipped cream and chocolate shavings. Throw a lid on the jar and it even travels well. Add some toasted hazelnuts on top for crunch or a dash of peppermint extract during the holidays.

---

2 cups heavy cream

½ vanilla bean, split lengthwise, or ½ teaspoon pure vanilla extract

3½ ounces semi-sweet dark chocolate

¼ cup espresso or strongly brewed coffee

½ cup natural cane sugar, divided

3 tablespoons cocoa powder

Pinch of sea salt

2 egg yolks, at room temperature

—

TOPPING

1 cup whipping cream

2 tablespoons confectioners' sugar

Place a rack in the middle of the oven and preheat to 300°F. In a saucepan over low heat, gently warm the heavy cream with the vanilla seeds until tiny bubbles form around the edges, about 8 minutes. In another bowl, break up the chocolate. Once the cream is hot, pour it over the chocolate into smallish pieces. Let it sit for 1 minute, then stir to incorporate until the mixture is even in color.

Clean out the saucepan, return it to medium heat and pour in the coffee and ⅓ cup of the sugar. Stir and cook for about 2 minutes, until the mixture is bubbling and the sugar is completely dissolved. Turn off the heat and whisk in the cocoa powder and sea salt. Add the chocolate cream to the coffee mixture and stir to mix well. In another bowl, whisk the yolks with the remaining 2 tablespoons sugar. Add a few spoonfuls of the warm cream to the yolks to temper them (keep them from cooking in the hot liquid), then add the warmed yolks to the pudding mixture. Stir well to combine. Strain the pudding through a fine-mesh sieve into a small pitcher or pouring vessel.

Divide the pudding evenly among 4 large or 6 smaller ramekins. Place them in a shallow baking dish and fill the dish halfway up the sides of the ramekins with

the sprouted kitchen bowl + spoon

water. Bake for 35 to 40 minutes. Let them chill in the fridge for at least 2 hours, and preferably overnight, to set.

Beat the whipping cream and confectioners' sugar until very soft peaks form. Serve each pudding with a generous dollop of the whipped cream. The pudding will keep, covered, for 5 days.

Key Lime Eton Mess

Serves 4

Before my infatuation with salads really set in, my dad and I would go on dates in search of the best Caesar salad. No matter what else we chose to eat, there was always a salad on trial. The same restaurant we settled on with the best Caesar also made a fabulous sweet and sour, bright green key lime pie. Now, I always choose the chocolate option on a dessert menu, but the tender memories I have with my Dad and that dessert, its graham crust, a custardy citrus filling, still attract me to the flavors of that classic pie. I have bastardized a classic Eton Mess here—an English dessert of whipped cream, meringues, and berries—by replacing the berries with a lime curd, and adding another crunchy, crumbly element to mimic the key lime pie crust.

The curd can be made a few days in advance. This recipe yields exactly the amount of curd you'll need for the dessert. If you want some leftover to spread on toast or to drape over a bowlful of berries, double the recipe—I highly suggest that you do. The curd will be yellow, despite the green we associate with limes, because of the yolk, butter, and natural lime juice. Because the whipped cream will soften the meringues as they sit, this is best served within 1 hour of assembling.

LIME CURD

1 egg

1 egg yolk

Zest of 1 lime

¼ cup plus 1 tablespoon freshly squeezed lime juice

¼ cup natural cane sugar

Sea salt

3 tablespoons unsalted butter, cubed

—

6 whole graham crackers, crushed to pea size (about 1⅓ cup)

¼ cup oats

3 tablespoons unsalted butter, at room temperature

2 tablespoons natural cane sugar

Pinch of salt

—

1 cup whipping cream

2 cups crushed meringues

Lime zest, for garnish

Place a fine-mesh strainer over a bowl and set aside. In a medium saucepan (not nonstick) over low heat, whisk together the egg, egg yolk, lime zest and juice, sugar, and salt. Add the butter, whisking constantly, until melted. Just barely increase the heat and cook over medium-low, whisking constantly, until the mixture thickens. It's done when you lift the whisk and the mixture holds some shape, like very loose pudding. Press the mixture through the strainer, cover, and set aside. This much can be done a few days in advance and stored in the refrigerator. Bring it to room temperature before using.

Place a rack in the middle of the oven and preheat to 350°F. In a bowl, combine the crushed graham crackers, oats, butter, sugar, and salt. Mix together with your fingertips so the butter evenly distributes. Spread on a baking sheet and bake for 15 minutes, stirring halfway through, until lightly browned. Cool completely and break up any large chunks.

Beat the whipping cream until loose peaks form; you don't want super-stiff—pillowy is nice here. Fold in the crumbled meringues and the lime curd, just once or twice, being careful not to overmix.

Arrange small bowls with a scoop of the whipped cream mixture, a few tablespoons of the crumble, and then repeat, finishing with a crumble layer and a garnish of lime zest. Chill for 30 minutes before serving.

Lemon Creams *with* Blueberries *and* Gingersnaps

Serves 4

I'm still amazed at the lightning speed at which this dessert comes together. I believe this cream—like a lighter and looser version of pudding—is the answer to your quick dessert repertoire. It almost reminds me of a richer yogurt—smooth and sweet, melts in your mouth, just tart enough to pair beautifully with fresh berries and a little something crunchy for good measure. Try to find Meyer lemons if you can, but a standard lemon will work just fine here. The Meyers have a thinner skin and sweeter flavor. A standard lemon will make these a little more tart, not necessarily a bad thing as it will balance sweetness. This is a light-tasting treat, despite the heavy cream—precisely the thing to finish a meal without feeling stuffed.

2 cups heavy cream

⅔ cup natural cane sugar

Zest of 1 Meyer lemon, plus more for garnish

4 to 5 tablespoons Meyer lemon juice

Sea salt

1½ cups fresh blueberries, washed and dried

4 to 5 crunchy gingersnap cookies

In a saucepan over medium heat, combine the cream, sugar, and lemon zest. Stir until the sugar dissolves. Bring the mixture to a simmer and cook for about 4 minutes, until there are bubbles around the edges and it has thickened. Turn off the heat and add the lemon juice and a small pinch of salt. Allow the mixture to cool completely. Strain it if you don't like zest or stray seeds.

Divide the lemon cream among 4 small ramekins or bowls and transfer to the fridge to set for at least 6 hours, preferably a full day to really set up.

When ready to serve, top them with a handful of fresh blueberries (I'll cut a few in half for texture), a crumble of the gingersnaps, a spoonful more berries, and lemon zest for garnish. Serve chilled.

Mixed Berry Tiramisu

Serves 6

My parents have always hosted barbecues in their backyard during the summer. My mom loves a party and they have a perfect space for it. When I first started showing an interest in cooking, I took the dessert assignment for the backyard parties because it seemed safest. I could find a dependable recipe and follow directions. The berry tiramisu idea came from an episode of *Everyday Italian* on the Food Network. I used to pour over those shows, taking notes and picking up tips. Maybe it's nostalgia, but I continue to make my own version, no recipe needed.

I consider this a bowl food because once you scoop out a portion, it's a bit of a mess and easier to eat from a bowl. I use a mix of berries—fresh when they're in season or frozen otherwise. The version below has some lemon zest in the cream layer, but replacing the citrus with shaved chocolate makes things a little more decadent. The liqueur contributes both flavor and a liquid to thin the jam so it saturates the ladyfingers. If you need a nonalcoholic alternative, fruit juice can stand in.

1½ cups raspberry jam

½ cup Chambord or other raspberry liqueur

2 tablespoons water

1½ pounds mixed berries, fresh or frozen

1½ cups light or heavy whipping cream

¾ cup mascarpone

3 tablespoons confectioners' sugar

½ teaspoon pure vanilla extract

Zest of 2 lemons

24 ladyfingers, give or take depending on pan

In a mixing bowl, combine the jam, liqueur, and water and mix well.

Cut the berries so they are similar sizes—blueberries and raspberries are fine as is, halve the cherries, and halve or quarter the strawberries. Set aside.

With an electric or stand mixer, whip the cream until loose peaks form. Add the mascarpone, confectioners' sugar, vanilla, and lemon zest and whip again just until firm peaks form.

In an 11- by 7-inch pan or 3-quart baking dish, spread a thin layer of the jam mixture. Arrange a single layer of ladyfingers to cover the bottom of the pan. Spread half of the jam mixture over the ladyfingers, being sure to liberally coat each cookie. Distribute three-quarters of the berries on top of the jam layer, and spread half of the cream evenly on top of the berries. Repeat with another layer of ladyfingers, the rest of the jam, and the remaining cream. Sprinkle the remaining berries on top. Let it rest for at least 6 hours in the fridge—this is best if made a full day in advance. Allow it to sit for 10 minutes at room temperature before serving.

Molten Cakes à la Mode

Serves 4

These are dangerously simple to make. Everything gets mixed together in one bowl, baked, and served within 15 minutes. If you're a chocolate fan, I don't need to sell you on a warm, gooey-centered cake. Plus, I think you likely already have all the items you need in your fridge and pantry.

Because these are pretty simple, I suggest using the best-quality chocolate and butter you can afford. It makes a difference. Depending on the season, a little mint extract and mint chip ice cream are my favorite flavor additions. In the summer, the cakes are excellent with vanilla bean ice cream and some berry coulis on top. And yes, they need to be in a bowl. The cold ice cream and warm cake make a bit of a mess, and you'll need the sides of the bowl to collect your perfectly proportioned scoopful.

½ cup unsalted butter, plus more for greasing

5 ounces semi-sweet dark chocolate, roughly chopped

½ cup natural cane sugar

2 eggs

2 egg yolks

2 tablespoons whole wheat pastry flour

Sea salt

Ice cream, for serving

Place a rack in the middle of the oven and preheat to 400°F. Lightly butter 4 (6- or 8-ounce) ramekins.

Set a glass bowl over a pot of simmering water. The bottom of the bowl should not touch the water line. Put the butter, chocolate, and sugar in the bowl and stir occasionally until melted and smooth. Remove from the heat.

In another bowl, whisk together the eggs and egg yolks. Add the eggs, flour, and a pinch of salt to the chocolate mixture and stir vigorously to mix well. Divide the mixture among the 4 ramekins. Place them on a baking sheet and bake for 10 to 14 minutes, until the tops are just dry. Let them rest for just a minute and then invert each cake into a small bowl. Top with a scoop of ice cream or topping of choice and enjoy immediately.

Peach Derby Ice Cream

Makes 1 quart

Peach ice cream will always remind me of my late grandfather. He had one of those ice cream makers you hand-crank and that needs rock salt to keep cool. My mom said he only made two flavors: vanilla or fresh peach in the summertime, which sounds very artisanal of him. Each time I make this, I go back and forth if it's better to put the peaches in the ice cream or leave them on top. To really taste the peach, I double the peaches and put half in and use the rest as a topping. I like them in the ice cream for the sake of convenience, but the peach flavor is more subdued when frozen, so I also throw a handful on top. I use part buttermilk to bring in the slightest bit of acidity, but it is very understated and makes this ice cream perfect for summer.

¾ cup plus 2 tablespoons whole milk

2 tablespoons cornstarch

1 cup heavy cream

2 tablespoons brown rice syrup

¾ cup natural cane sugar

Pinch of salt

⅓ cup mascarpone, at room temperature

1 cup buttermilk

¼ teaspoon pure vanilla extract

½ teaspoon cinnamon

2 tablespoons bourbon

½ cup toasted, chopped pecans, plus more for garnish

2 ripe peaches, pitted and diced

Mix the 2 tablespoons of the milk with the cornstarch in a small bowl to make a smooth slurry.

Combine the remaining milk, the cream, brown rice syrup, and sugar in a large saucepan or pot (at least 4 quarts). Bring the mixture to a very gentle simmer over low heat and cook, stirring occasionally to dissolve the sugar, about 3 minutes. Remove from the heat and whisk in the cornstarch mixture.

Bring the mixture back to a simmer and cook, stirring constantly, another minute.

Gradually whisk in the mascarpone until smooth. Stir in the buttermilk, vanilla, cinnamon, and bourbon. Chill the mixture in the refrigerator for two hours or until cold. If it chills too long, a fat layer will separate to the top. Remove this solid piece before churning.

Churn the ice cream according to the manufacturer's directions. In the last minutes, add the toasted pecans and half the peaches. Spoon the mixture into a storage container and freeze until firm.

Top your scoops of ice cream with a sprinkle of fresh peaches and more pecans.

the sprouted kitchen bowl + spoon

Roasted Pears in Goat Milk Caramel (Cajeta)

Serves 4

If you don't make these pears, you must at least try the cajeta. I am not typically a caramel fan—usually it's toothache-sweet—but this goat milk caramel is sweet without being cloyingly so, and complements the warm fruit perfectly. The cajeta recipe yields about 1 ½ cups, more than you'll need for this treat, but it makes a great dip for apple slices or stirred into hot coffee. If you are a stickler for smoothness, strain the caramel mixture when it's finished cooking (though I don't find this step necessary).

CARAMEL

4 cups goat milk

1 scant cup natural cane sugar

1 cinnamon stick

½ teaspoon baking soda

1 teaspoon water

¼ teaspoon sea salt

—

2 pears, ripe but still firm

2 tablespoons grapeseed or other neutral oil

1 tablespoon honey

½ vanilla bean, split lengthwise, or 1 teaspoon pure vanilla extract

⅓ cup chopped pistachio nuts

2 tablespoons old-fashioned oats

Vanilla bean ice cream, for serving (optional)

In a large pot (preferably a Dutch oven) over medium heat, combine the goat milk, sugar, and cinnamon stick and bring to a simmer, stirring occasionally, until the sugar is dissolved. In a ramekin, dissolve the baking soda in the water. When the milk has bubbles around the edge, remove it from the heat, add the baking soda mixture, and stir. Return the pot to the heat and bring the mixture to a very gentle boil. Cook for 50 to 60 minutes, stirring occasionally, until it's reduced to a pale golden color. Remove the cinnamon stick. Turn the heat up slightly and continue to stir frequently as the mixture begins to thicken, being sure to mix well so the sugar doesn't burn, 10 to 15 minutes. The mixture should be the consistency of a thick maple syrup—keep in mind it will firm up as it cools. If the mixture seems too thin, keep cooking. Otherwise, remove it from the heat and stir in the salt. The cajeta will keep for 1 month, covered, in the fridge.

Preheat the oven to 375°F. Slice the pears in half and remove the core, making a small well. Arrange the pears on a rimmed baking sheet, cut-side up. Rub a thin layer of oil on the cut side of the pears, about ½ tablespoon total, and bake for 18 to 20 minutes until soft and the edges are just golden. Mix the remaining

1½ tablespoons oil, the honey, and vanilla bean seeds in a small bowl to combine. Add the pistachios and oats and toss everything to coat. Spread the nut mixture on a parchment-lined baking sheet and bake for 15 to 18 minutes, stirring occasionally, until toasted.

Serve each bowl with a few spoonfuls of the caramel, a roasted pear half, and a spoonful of the nut crumble nestled into the core of each pear. Add a scoop of vanilla ice cream if you're feeling decadent.

Grapefruit Lillet Sherbet

Makes 1 quart

A sherbet or sorbet always has a place in my bowl during the summer months when all I want is something cold and light. Lillet is an apéritif that is a blend of wine, brandy, fruits, and herbs. It's a unique ingredient to have in your cocktail repertoire, and it also gives this sherbet a more interesting flavor; make the sherbet kid friendly by simply leaving it out. I love the super-tart grapefruit here, but if you're looking for a more mellow citrus flavor, tangerine or blood orange juice makes a great substitute.

This mixture also makes excellent popsicles.

3 cups freshly squeezed grapefruit juice	¾ cup half-and-half
Zest of 1 grapefruit	¼ cup Lillet
1 cup plus 2 tablespoons natural cane sugar	1 tablespoon finely chopped mint leaves

Heat 1 cup of the juice, the zest, and the sugar in a small saucepan until the sugar is dissolved. Transfer it to a bowl with the rest of the juice and chill in the fridge for 1 to 2 hours or until completely cool. Stir in the half-and-half and Lillet, pour the chilled mixture into your ice cream maker, and run according to the manufacturer's instructions. In the last 2 minutes, add the mint.

Transfer to a freezer-safe container and freeze to desired firmness, 3 to 4 hours. Note that after a full day, the sherbet will become quite hard. Let it sit at room temperature for 5 minutes before trying to scoop.

Cocoa Banana Cups

My beloved college roommate and I shared the struggle of loving treats and trying to eat healthy. When you're coming up with snacks in a dorm room where the only appliance is a microwave, options are limited. In a coffee mug, we would mash up a ripe banana, throw in a sprinkle of chocolate chips and a scoop of peanut butter and mash it all together. With just a blitz in the microwave to warm it up and melt the chocolate, that treat never got old. It still doesn't, but I tried to make it a touch lovelier to look at here.

To get a smooth pudding-like texture, ideally you'll want to use a high-powered blender, but a food processor can pull it off as well.

This recipe can be made with natural peanut butter, hazelnut butter, or whatever nut butter you have on hand. Most of the sweetness comes from the banana, so wait until yours are extra-ripe with lots of brown spots, when they have the most natural sugars.

---

2 large, overripe bananas

2 tablespoons maple syrup

¼ cup natural cocoa powder

⅓ cup almond butter

¼ to ⅓ cup nondairy milk (almond, rice, or coconut)

Sea salt

Banana slices and toasted almonds, for garnish

In a high-powered blender, combine the bananas, maple syrup, cocoa, almond butter, nondairy milk, and a pinch of salt. Blend just until smooth, adding the milk as needed.

Transfer to small ramekins or bowls and chill for at least 1 hour before eating.

Garnish with chopped banana and toasted almonds.

From left to right: Tahini Citrus Miso Dressing, Everyday Green Dressing, Maple Balsamic Dressing, and SK Sriracha

DRESSINGS AND SAUCES

What grains are in the cupboard? Which vegetables need to be used up? Which protein have you not burned out on lately? Creativity often lies in making do with what you have, what's in season, or what you can afford. Having a grasp on a few different dressings and sauces can turn a bowl of grains, vegetables, and protein or legumes into something worth calling dinner. You can make them creamy, bright, and full of citrus, like the **Tahini Citrus Miso Dressing** (page 203). I generally pick a flavor profile, make sure there are lots of fresh herbs, a touch of sweetness, salinity, and spice plus a good ratio of acidity. When you find what tastes best to you, with just a little confidence, some chopping, and a whisk (or a quick blitz in a food processor or blender), experimenting becomes second nature.

Dark Cherry Hazelnut Salsa

Makes 2 cups

I serve this salsa with blue corn chips, toss it in a quesadilla with soft goat cheese, or warm it briefly and put it on grilled fish or chicken for a stunning topping. Cherries have a short season, but if you grab them while they're good, this is a great way to highlight their tart sweetness. I will do everything in a food processor for a finer salsa, but you could chop by hand if you like a more coarse texture. The amount of heat here depends largely on how many seeds you leave in the serrano—remove them all for an extra-mild salsa.

3 tablespoons minced shallot or red onion

1 small serrano chile, stemmed and seeded to taste

Zest and juice of 1 lime

¼ cup toasted, chopped hazelnuts

⅓ cup chopped cilantro

2 cups (about ¾ pound) cherries, pitted and halved

Sea salt and freshly ground pepper

In a food processor, add the shallot, chile, lime zest and juice, hazelnuts, and cilantro and pulse a few times until well chopped. Add the cherries, a couple pinches of salt and pepper and pulse a few more times just to chop and combine.

Taste for salt and pepper and keep covered in the fridge until ready to use.

Everyday Green Dressing

Makes 2 cups

This recipe got its name because it's the answer to all of my quick, "everyday," throw-together meals. It's my favorite salad dressing for green salads. I also use it to drizzle on top of any sort of roasted vegetables, as a dip for sweet potato wedges, or stirred into cooked grains for a flavor boost. It's super light and doesn't compete with other parts of your meal. Mix and match your herbs based on what is on hand. Basil should be the dominant herb and then from there, I use what I have—sometimes a bit of tarragon, chives, or dill, maybe in addition to, or to replace, the cilantro if I know I'll be sharing with someone who has an aversion to it. It would be hard to overdo the greenery here.

It has more of a salad dressing consistency, especially with juicy lemons. If you know you are going to want it thicker, say for the dipping route, a tablespoon or two of good-quality mayonnaise will thicken it.

2 cloves garlic	1 tablespoon honey
3 green onions, white and green parts	2 teaspoons apple cider vinegar
2 tablespoons drained capers	1 cup whole Greek yogurt
½ teaspoon sea salt	¼ cup grated Parmesan cheese
½ teaspoon freshly ground pepper	2 cups firmly packed basil leaves
¼ teaspoon red pepper flakes	¾ cup flat-leaf parsley
Zest and juice of 2 lemons, preferably Meyer	1 cup cilantro
	¼ cup extra-virgin olive oil

In a food processor, pulse the garlic, green onions, capers, salt, pepper, red pepper flakes, zest and juice of the lemons, and honey to combine. Add the cider vinegar, yogurt, Parmesan, basil, parsley, cilantro, and, with the motor running, drizzle in the olive oil. Taste and add more seasonings, vinegar, or oil to taste. The dressing will keep, covered, in the fridge for 1 week.

Pantry Peanut Sauce

Makes 1½ cups

No storebought peanut sauce is as tasty as this one, which you can likely put together simply with pantry staples. It hits all the salty, sweet marks and needs nothing more than a good buzz in the processor or blender. Keep it on the thicker side for a sauce or spread, or thin it out with a little more rice vinegar for a salad dressing or dip.

2 cloves garlic	1 tablespoon rice vinegar
3 tablespoons freshly grated ginger	2 teaspoons toasted sesame oil
Zest and juice of 2 limes	¾ cup creamy peanut butter
½ teaspoon red pepper flakes	2 to 4 tablespoons light coconut milk or water, to thin
2 tablespoons honey	¼ cup chopped cilantro (optional)
3 tablespoons soy sauce or tamari	

Add the garlic, ginger, lime zest and juice, pepper flakes, honey, soy sauce, vinegar, sesame oil, and peanut butter to a blender or food processor and blend until completely smooth. Add the coconut milk, 1 tablespoon at a time, until you reach the desired consistency, keeping in mind it will thicken in the fridge. Pulse in the cilantro. Keep the sauce stored in a covered container in the fridge for up to 2 weeks.

Maple Balsamic Dressing

The measurements given here offer a moderate amount of dressing, but everything may be doubled. The maple syrup adds a curious sweetness to the assertive balsamic vinegar, and you're left with a dressing that's good on just about anything. I put it on roasted winter squash, carrots, and asparagus most often.

1 small shallot, finely minced	¼ teaspoon dried Italian herbs
2 tablespoons maple syrup	2 tablespoons balsamic vinegar
1 teaspoon Dijon mustard	¼ cup extra-virgin olive oil
¼ teaspoon sea salt	

In a small bowl, whisk together the shallot, maple syrup, mustard, salt, Italian herbs, and vinegar. Drizzle in the olive oil while continuing to whisk. Taste, and add additional salt, if needed. The dressing will keep covered in the fridge for 1 week.

SK Sriracha

We went a very long time without having "rooster sauce" in the house, but once the gateway bottle made its way in, I knew Hugh was hooked on the spicy condiment. A few ingredients I don't recognize and its lengthy shelf life got me thinking a more wholesome version was possible. It's so easy, takes all of 10 minutes, and makes a great edible gift, too. The heat factor is different every time because hot chiles are unpredictable. Always spicy, but sometimes, especially the homegrown sort, are make-your-eyes-water hot. The bell pepper mellows the heat just enough for those of us who don't want to burn our mouths off. I use coconut oil, but the aroma does come through in the finished sauce. If you don't want any essence of coconut, choose another high-heat, neutral-tasting oil.

---

2 teaspoons coconut oil

½ pound (about 2) red bell peppers or other mild peppers, stemmed

½ pound hot chiles (red jalapeño, serrano, Thai), stemmed and barely seeded

5 cloves garlic

3 tablespoons coconut sugar (or muscovado or brown sugar)

2 tablespoons soy sauce or tamari

¼ cup rice wine vinegar

Sea salt

In a large heavy skillet, heat the coconut oil over medium-high heat. Roughly chop the peppers and chiles. To the hot pan, add the bell peppers, chiles, and garlic and sauté for about 5 minutes, until softened. Add the sugar, soy sauce, and vinegar and cook 1 minute longer for the sugar to dissolve. Turn off the heat and allow everything to cool, stirring the mixture occasionally to release pockets of steam.

Transfer to a food processor and let it run until the mixture is smooth. Add salt to taste. This sauce will keep about 3 weeks, covered, in the fridge.

Tahini Citrus Miso Dressing

Makes about 1 cup

One would think the miso here would pigeonhole this as an Asian dressing, but not so. Instead, the miso offers an incredible depth of flavor and salinity, so truly this dressing works on just about anything. I love it on the Herbed Falafel (page 115), but it's also my go-to for a basic kale salad with all sorts of shredded vegetables. Tahini and miso should be easy to find at a health food store or any larger supermarket with an international section.

½ cup tahini

2 tablespoons white or yellow miso

2 tablespoons honey

1 tablespoon toasted sesame oil

2 teaspoons Sriracha or hot sauce

1 tablespoon rice wine vinegar

Juice of 1 large orange (about ⅓ cup)

Sea salt and freshly ground pepper

Lemon juice, to taste

In a mixing bowl, whisk together the tahini, miso, honey, sesame oil, and Sriracha to combine. Whisk in the vinegar, orange juice, salt, and pepper to taste. Thin with water or lemon juice, 1 tablespoon at a time, if needed. Taste and adjust seasoning. The dressing will keep, covered, in the fridge for 2 weeks.

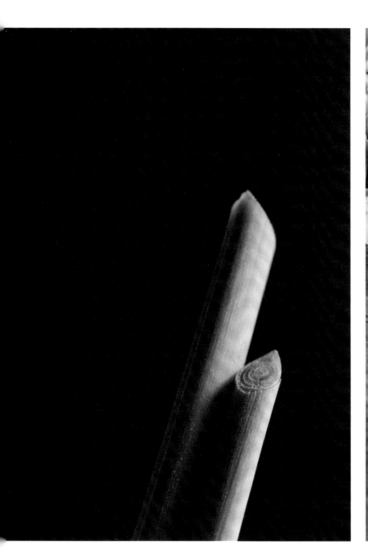

Thai Lemongrass Sauce

Makes 1 cup

I love Thai flavors, but I don't have an ethnic market nearby that sources some of the special ingredients that make the dishes so unique. So, for me, cooking authentic Thai food is not something that happens often around here. This sauce is how I get my fix. It's fresh, full of lemongrass, and spicy from a good nub of ginger and a hot chile. The heat of chiles varies so much that I hate to qualify the spice level here. If you want a burn, leave all the seeds in (you're crazy) and if you want it mild, remove all the ribs and seeds completely. I have used a jalapeño here for a more predictable, while not authentic, milder heat.

I make rice bowls with grilled shrimp or fish, veggies, and warm this sauce to drizzle on top. It's thin, but still brings all the flavor you need. It could be the base for a soup or the liquid to steam your favorite fish en papillote.

---

2 stalks lemongrass, trimmed, outer layer removed

2 teaspoons coconut oil

2 cloves garlic

1 small shallot

½ teaspoon cumin

3 tablespoons freshly grated ginger or galangal

1 green chile (Thai or jalapeño)

Zest and juice of 2 limes

¾ teaspoon sea salt

1 small bunch cilantro

½ cup coconut milk

2 tablespoons sesame oil

Crush the lemongrass stalks with the side of a knife and coarsely chop. In a small pan, warm the coconut oil over medium heat. Add the lemongrass, garlic, and shallot and sauté for 1 to 2 minutes until just softened and fragrant. In a food processor, combine the sautéed lemongrass mixture with the cumin, ginger, green chile (seeds removed if you prefer less heat), lime zest and juice, and salt. Run the processor to combine completely. Add the cilantro, coconut milk, and sesame oil and run the processor 1 minute longer to combine. Taste and adjust seasoning, if necessary.

Sauce will keep, covered, in the fridge for 1 week, but note that heat will intensify slightly over time.

Crème Fraîche

When small containers of crème fraîche cost as much as they do at the market, it's tough to beat making your own. Think of it as yogurt's more decadent relative. It makes pasta dishes smooth and silky, is delicious stirred into soft scrambled eggs, and makes a tasty dip for fresh strawberries when mixed with a bit of muscovado sugar and cardamom. You'll want to use unpasteurized or vat-pasteurized cream if you can (it works with pasteurized cream, it just takes longer to thicken).

1 cup heavy cream	2 tablespoons buttermilk

In a glass bowl or pitcher, combine the cream and buttermilk. Cover with a dish towel and let sit at room temperature to culture and thicken, 18 to 24 hours. Cover and chill in the fridge. The crème fraîche stores well in the fridge for 1 week.

Yogurt Ranch Dressing

Makes 2 cups

Whatever my mom threw together for dinner when we were kids, without fail there were also cut-up cucumbers and tomatoes with ranch dressing on them as our "salad." We never complained; kids love ranch. I may have more diverse tastes these days, but a Bibb lettuce salad with farm tomatoes, avocado, and homemade ranch is a simple pleasure. Don't be scared of mayonnaise; it's simply eggs and oil, and the dressing needs it to emulsify. You can make this dressing with a vegan mayonnaise as well. I whip this together in a food processor, but it also can be whisked by hand in a bowl.

1 large clove garlic

3 green onions, white and green parts, roughly chopped

2 tablespoons chopped fresh flat-leaf parsley

1 teaspoon dried oregano

1 tablespoon Dijon mustard

1 tablespoon extra-virgin olive oil

1 tablespoon lemon zest

2 tablespoons freshly squeezed lemon juice

½ cup good-quality mayonnaise or veganaise

½ cup full-fat Greek yogurt

¼ cup buttermilk

1 teaspoon sea salt

½ teaspoon freshly ground pepper

In the bowl of a food processor, combine the garlic, green onions, parsley, oregano, mustard, and oil and pulse a few times until well chopped. Add the lemon zest and juice, mayonnaise, yogurt, buttermilk, salt, and pepper and blend until smooth. Transfer to a container and refrigerate for at least 1 hour for the flavors to develop. The dressing will keep, covered, in the fridge for 1 week.

Roasted Pasilla *and* Goat Cheese Sauce

Makes 1½ cups

Whenever I don't feel like cooking, I have tacos or taco-type bowls because they're really just about assembly. This sauce is the perfect accompaniment; the goat cheese is creamy and tangy, and the peppers and cilantro are fresh tasting. It's exactly the sort of sauce I love to have on hand when I'm dressing up something simple. It also makes an interesting dip on a veggie tray.

½ small red onion, peeled	¼ teaspoon cayenne pepper
2 pasilla peppers	Juice of 1 lemon
⅓ cup extra-virgin olive oil	2 tablespoons white wine vinegar
⅓ cup toasted pepitas (pumpkin seeds)	¼ cup water
4 ounces soft goat cheese (chèvre)	1 cup coarsely chopped cilantro
1 teaspoon honey	1 teaspoon sea salt
½ teaspoon chili powder	½ teaspoon freshly ground pepper

Preheat the broiler. Rub the peppers and onion with a drizzle of olive oil. Place them on a baking sheet and broil them for 12 to 15 minutes until charred and collapsed. Let cool, then rub off the skin of the peppers and remove the stems and seeds.

In a food processor, combine the onion and pasillas, the remaining olive oil, the pepitas, goat cheese, honey, chili powder, cayenne, lemon juice, and vinegar and process until combined. Add the water, cilantro, salt, and pepper and give it another pulse. Taste for seasonings, adding a pinch more cayenne if you'd like it spicier.

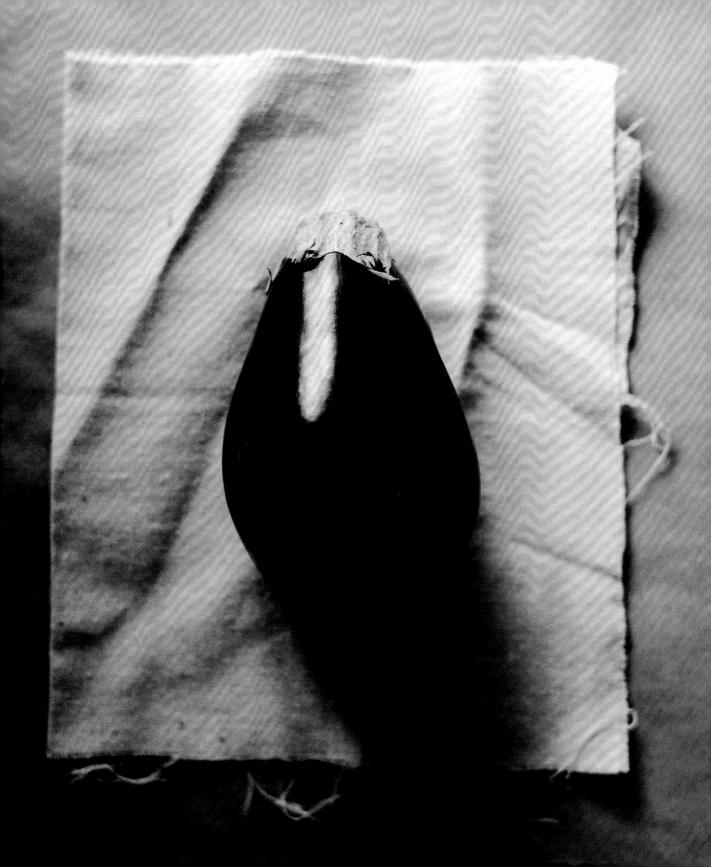

With Gratitude

While never my long-term plan, writing cookbooks has been equally the most rewarding and challenging process I've worked through. I've found that God's plan for my career has made me stronger, more humble, and more generous and hospitable due to the surplus of food that goes through our kitchen. I love that this is part of my story.

Hugh, it makes me smile when I think of the food critic I've made of you in this project. The man who could happily survive on cheeseburgers and breakfast burritos can also tell me when a dressing needs a pinch more sweetness or argues that the apples in a crisp are superior when cut in cubes rather than in wedges. Who knew? I am so grateful for your feedback but even more so blown away by the talent you have in capturing the images of the recipes included here. You make it so much more than pictures of food. I am proud of what we've created together.

My trusted team of testers: Mary Jo Boyd-Prince, Mollie Forte, Courtney LeDuc, Susan Turner, Stacy Ladenburger, Sarah Kieffer, Erin Gianopoulos, Adriana Lukasik, Ali Slagle, Ariana Christoffers, Grace Rusch, and a few others who pinch-hit at the end. Thank you!

To the entire team at Ten Speed Press who helped me make a niche idea, an entire book. My editor, Jenny Wapner, who graciously led me to define this idea and make sense of the words that jumble in my head. Thank you Tatiana, for your hard work and beautiful design.

My family and closest friends—those who kept interested in my project and encouraged me. Thank you for eating with us, standing in as models, taking leftovers, and reminding me that it's pretty awesome that this is my job.

And lastly, to blog readers and *Sprouted Kitchen* cheerleaders. You're the reason I keep at this and why all the time cleaning dishes is worth it one hundred times over. Thank you for your kind words, comments, emails, and support. I feel like I have hundreds of friends I simply haven't met, and that's pretty damn wonderful.

About Us

SARA FORTE fell in love with food while working on an organic farm during college in San Luis Obispo. She followed that passion to Italy to work at a bed-and-breakfast and olive oil farm, then for a few caterers, markets, and is now the creator of the blog, *Sprouted Kitchen* (sproutedkitchen.com) and cookbook author. As a health-focused cook, she is driven to share recipes for approachable, whole foods that are perfectly suited to the everyday home cook. Her work has been featured in *Martha Stewart*, *Whole Living*, *Every Day with Rachel Ray*, *Sunset*, *InStyle*, *Redbook*, *Food and Wine*, and *Bon Appétit*. *Sprouted Kitchen* was awarded Best Food Blog by *Saveur* magazine for both Best Original Recipes and Best Photography. Sara currently does freelance recipe development, small catering events, and works as a personal chef. She spends her free time speed walking with girlfriends, tending a Pilates habit, and enjoying beach picnics with family and friends. Hugh and Sara live with their son, Curran, in Southern California.

HUGH FORTE is a photographer whose work is inspired by traveling and the desire to document personal, beautiful moments playing out in the world around him. While he is primarily wedding and lifestyle photographer, he created *Sprouted Kitchen* as a gift to Sara so they would have a shared creative outlet. With an attraction to light, color and texture, Hugh's eye is the perfect match for Sara's fresh cooking style. Hugh's dream day consists of reading books, riding waves, perfecting an excellent cup of coffee, and making his son laugh.

Index

Published in the United States by Ten Speed Press, an imprint
of the Crown Publishing Group, a division of Random House
LLC, a Penguin Random House Company, New York.
www.crownpublishing.com
www.tenspeed.com

Ten Speed Press and the Ten Speed Press colophon are
registered trademarks of Random House LLC.

Library of Congress Cataloging-in-Publication Data

Forte, Sara.
  The sprouted kitchen bowl and spoon : simple and inspired
whole foods recipes to savor and share / Sara Forte ;
photography by Hugh Forte. -- First edition.
      pages cm
    ISBN 978-1-60774-655-3
1. Cooking (Natural foods) 2. Salads. I. Title.
    TX741.F6673 2015
    641.3'02--dc23
                                           2014036843

Printed in China

Design by Tatiana Pavlova

10 9 8 7 6 5 4 3 2 1

First Edition